PENGUIN BUSINESS
WHY I STOPPED WEARING MY SOCKS

Born and brought up in Mumbai, Alok Kejriwal is a serial digital entrepreneur and is currently the CEO and co-founder of Games2win. His first two companies, contests2win.com and Mobile2win, pioneered digital gaming and promotions in the world. Mobile2win was later acquired by the Walt Disney Co. Besides being a businessperson, Alok is also a passionate speaker and a mentor for emerging entrepreneurs. Alok has spoken at over 100 conferences, including at venues such as the Wharton School and Harvard Business School, and many of the IIMs and IITs.

   Website: http://therodinhoods.com
   Twitter: https://twitter.com/rodinhood
   LinkedIn: https://www.linkedin.com/in/alokkejriwal/
   Instagram: https://www.instagram.com/rodinhood/
   Email: alok@rodinhood.com

WHY I STOPPED WEARING MY SOCKS

ALOK KEJRIWAL

PENGUIN
BUSINESS

An imprint of Penguin Random House

PENGUIN BUSINESS

USA | Canada | UK | Ireland | Australia
New Zealand | India | South Africa | China | Singapore

Penguin Business is part of the Penguin Random House group of companies
whose addresses can be found at global.penguinrandomhouse.com

Published by Penguin Random House India Pvt. Ltd
4th Floor, Capital Tower 1, MG Road,
Gurugram 122 002, Haryana, India

Penguin
Random House
India

First published by Westland Publications Private Limited in 2018
Published in Penguin Business by Penguin Random House India 2022

ISBN 9780143459088

Typeset in Arno Pro by SÜRYA, New Delhi

Printed at Repro India Limited

www.penguin.co.in

Offered at the lotus feet of:
Gurudev Sri Sri Ravi Shankar, Mahavatar Babaji and
Lord Bankey Bihari of Vrindavan
Dedicated to Chhavi, Nana, Anushka, Amaya

CONTENTS

Introduction

Two days after my gruelling tenth-grade exams, when I was all of sixteen, I began working in the family business or should I say family businesses, that were all based in Mumbai. For the next twelve years, I worked with my father, grandfather and grandmother. My father owned a factory that manufactured socks. My grandfather ran a transport business. And my grandmother traded on the stock market!

That my father and grandfather were businesspeople was no surprise. It was almost the norm in our community. Their lives revolved round their work. But my grandmother was a path-breaker of sorts. Largely self-taught, her being in business was something of a surprise. More about that later.

My life in business began among these people.

At sixteen, you don't get to choose what kind of work you do. And even more so in your family business. Hence, over the next few years, I did a variety of things. I co-ordinated the transport of all kinds of goods for my grandfather, oversaw the manufacture of countless pairs of socks for my father and answered tricky stock market questions for my grandmother. I was the quintessential, sincere, dedicated Marwari 'chhora' (boy) until something unexpected appeared in my life—the Internet!

The Bombay (it hadn't yet become Mumbai) that I grew up in was magical. There was a palpable, buzzing business energy that pervaded the city. Hugging the ocean was the elite business district Nariman Point where formally dressed men holding black and maroon briefcases darted in and out of office buildings and banks doing business deals. They were the investment bankers and the stock, commodity and currency traders who made 'killlings' in their glass offices overlooking the Arabian Sea. In the evenings, in popular pubs along Marine Drive, you could spot the who's who of finance hanging out with their teams and clients. The Oberoi Hotel health club was the 'ultimate power hub'. Even as you relaxed in the sauna or the steamroom, there was the possibility that you could get an update or a stock 'tip' that could make you a fortune.

The diamond traders who lived on Walkeshwar and worked at Opera House were a class apart. In the morning, they walked barefoot, like renunciates to their temples to offer prayers. In the afternoon, the same people exchanged diamond 'puriyas' (pouches) worth crores amongst each other, based on a handshake. If you lived in South Bombay, being asked, 'Are you in diamonds?' was as common as being asked your name.

The Lower Parel area where the mills were located was where the 'industrialists' operated from. In the mornings, near the Mahalaxmi Station bridge, you could spot the Mercedes cars of the tycoons, driven by stiff chauffeurs, sporting white caps and gloves. Quite like in Bollywood movies, these powerful businessmen operated massive factories in and around the Parel area that employed thousands of workers who worked in eight-hour shifts and produced cloth, yarn and textile products for the local and export markets. The Bombay I grew up in was powerfully magnetic and radiated an aura of money, power, ambition and glory. I was completely spellbound by it and hoped to make my own place in it some day.

When my career began, my life seemed perfectly scripted. For the foreseeable future, that I would work in the family business was almost non-negotiable. But a near-catastrophic business event, combined with what I believe was divine intervention gave me a super-hot, crazy idea called contests2win.com. That website and other related businesses made me an early Indian internet entrepreneur. Now for more than two decades since that life-changing event, I have rejoiced in the extraordinary world of startups, venture capitalists and entrepreneurs. I've been laughed at by clients and family, bullied by senior government officers, been called a liar many times, made personal blunders ... and also seen real magic happen!

My adventures in China created a company that was acquired by Walt Disney. A surprise success in India had a VC greenmail me. These events, combined with the good fortune of meeting over seven thousand people up, close and personal, coupled with relentless pavement-pounding have taught me invaluable business lessons that I believe might be valuable for others too.

For the past few years, I have been active on social media. My articles and posts have received a very enthusiastic response. Overwhelming demand from friends and social media followers to curate and compile my most exciting stories has been the prime motivation for me to write this book. Each story in the pages that follow is real and true. The takeaways at the end of each story are my reflections. I believe they can be lessons for everyone.

I hope you enjoy reading my stories and their lessons as much as I have enjoyed writing them for you!

The Paranoia of Money

When I was born, my mother was nineteen years old, and my father, twenty-six. I was their first born (two sisters followed later). Interestingly, my Nani (maternal grandmother) and Nana (maternal grandfather) were themselves barely fifty. This setup was the classic Marwari family production cycle at work!

My Nani was a key influencer in my life. She told me often, 'Munna (my pet name), the moment you were born, the nurse came running to me and said, "It's a Baba ... a Baba (boy)!" I became very excited on hearing that and I forgot all the telephone numbers of our family members. So, it took me a while to contact them and tell them the good news.'

In case you missed it, the keyword was 'boy'. My mother was the only child of my grandparents. My Nani had always wanted a son, but that was not to be. I was the boy she had long prayed for. The day I was born, my Nani took charge of me, and I began living with my grandparents, about a mile away from my parental home.

My grandparents were the best parents I could have wished for. They were mature, easy-going, straightforward people who pretty much devoted themselves to raising me. My success and happiness was the only thing that mattered to them, and that in turn motivated me to make them very proud of me.

My Nani was obsessed with business. I think this was linked to her own family background. While her father was a senior government officer, all her uncles and cousins were very successful business people. She was motivated to be as wealthy and powerful as them versus being 'hand to mouth' as she would call being in a 'naukri'. My Nani's marriage to my Nana, a businessman, aided her instant and seamless entry into the world of business.

Often at dinner time, she would greet me by saying '*Aaj market mein aag lag gayee!*' The market was on fire today (It has dramatically risen!). Sometimes it would be, '*Market pura barbaad ho gaya*' (It has sharply fallen!). The market was ruined today. By market, she meant the stock market. She was obsessed with money and spent her entire adult life hoarding it. Most conversations in my early childhood were about business, contracts, trade, failed deals and so on.

My Nani often blamed my Nana for being a lousy businessman. My Nana had a transport business. In my Nani's opinion, he was not aggressive enough and took life a bit too easy. Her favourite was 'Your Nana has no running income.' Running income to her meant a predictable monthly sum of money like a monthly salary. I doubt any businessman has such a 'running income'. But anyway, that was my Nani's view.

It's important to point out that my Nani was not a negative person. On the contrary, she was very spiritual and worldly-wise. However, her mind was obsessed with hoarding wealth. All through my formative years in school and college, I grew up with the feeling that we didn't have enough money. The paranoia of not having money slowly began to embed itself deep within me, and I believe that my drive, restlessness, and ambition spring from this fear. This paranoia made me constantly compete with myself, even when it was not needed. It made me try and over achieve, and still strive for more. I became obsessed with proving myself over and over again. I still have that paranoia and it pretty much drives me every single day!

The truth of the matter was that my Nana was actually a terrific businessman and is in fact, one of the most successful businessmen I have known. A migrant from the dusty town of Mathura in Uttar Pradesh, my Nana (with my Nani) came to Mumbai in search of a better life and to create wealth for himself and his family. A consummate and very affable networker, my Nana could easily establish relationships with diverse people and strike all kinds of deals with them! He traded in chemicals, exported snacks to Kuwait and Saudi Arabia, textiles to Pakistan, and leased compressors to be used for road construction. His transport business lasted the longest and caused most of the arguments at home. As a 'happy-go-lucky' person, my Nana was taken advantage of many times by his employees and partners. My Nani on the other hand was very strict and stern and would often direct my Nana to be tough and ruthless in his work from her armchair. It never worked. My Nana was sweet and thoughtful by nature and I believe those were the very same qualities that helped him garner his wealth and status.

My Nana grew his wealth discreetly and with a prudence that would make Warren Buffett proud. For instance, he bought most of the blue-chip stocks listed on the Bombay Stock Exchange (BSE) in their early days and never sold them. My Nana-Nani's relationship was the most unique I have seen. My Nani was hopelessly devoted to my Nana as a dedicated wife and life partner, but when it came to business, they often behaved like sworn enemies. How I wish my Nani had acknowledged my Nana's business acumen for what it truly was!

MY LEARNINGS

As parents, we must remember that our conduct, fears, aspirations, prejudices, desires, and preferences all get passed on to our children. Even when things may not be going well, we must try and not expose our paranoias and deep-seated regrets to our children. In my case, I channelised my inherited paranoia of 'not having enough money' positively into developing a relentless and ambitious drive, but things could just as well have gone the other way and I could have become a very negative person. I believe that we must expose our kids to our best side as much as possible. Our worst fears must stay hidden within us. We must deal with them, of course, but quietly.

My First Job

I was very good in studies and always ranked amongst the top ten students in my school. Then, as now, the Class X academic year was an extremely taxing one.

I completed my Class X exams on a sunny Friday in the March of 1985. I was looking forward to taking some time off. But that was not to be. My Nani now said, 'You've worked very hard, so take the Saturday and Sunday off and start working with Nana from Monday.' And that was that!

On Monday morning, I was in my Nana's office in a rundown building in the centre of South Mumbai. He ran a small transport company, and there was actually very little for me to do there. My Nani always complained that my Nana never reviewed his accounts and so I began inspecting his financial books to find possible errors and omissions in them.

One day, I asked him, 'Nana, why don't we grow our business? Why are we stuck to just a couple of corporate contracts when there are so many companies out there we can do business with?'

My Nana's reply was, 'Of course. We must! Why don't you start looking for more business?'

This was an open invitation for me to try my hand at business development. I was a naive teenager with a direct mandate from the owner to get new business, and I was all fired up! Sitting in the office, I tracked small and large corporations whose names I read in the financial newspapers and cold-called them for meetings. Most companies did not respond to me, but a few did and appointments were fixed. My Nana accompanied me to those meetings initially, and later, I began meeting potential customers on my own. Time passed. I joined college, but I was no longer just a student. I was also a working man.

One day, I heard about this concept called 'ODC'. It was an acronym for Odd Dimensional Cargo. My Nana's staff told me that ODC were opportunities for the most lucrative margins in the transport business. When equipment for large industrial plants came into the Mumbai docks, their odd shapes and package sizes required customised transportation services. Unlike for other goods, there were no fixed rates for the transport of these goods. For example, there was no standard cost to transport a fifty-foot furnace from Mumbai to Goa. ODC transporters would therefore charge irrational sums for their services and make huge profits.

I was so inspired that I called all the truck owners who supplied ODC vehicles and equipment in Mumbai and compiled an exhaustive database of them. I was confident that I too could get into this business.

A few months later, one of our close relatives Mr Navneet Zalani began working in the Ruchi Soya Group. They were setting up a massive new steel mill in Indore. I spoke to him and convinced him to introduce me to people within his company. I then liaised with the group's logistics team, pitched hard, drew detailed charts of my transportation plans, and snagged their ODC order! I was just eighteen years old. In the months that followed, I single-handedly transported most of the heavy machinery and equipment that National Steel Industries in Indore runs on today. When the steel plant went live, I was heartily congratulated by my Nana and by many folks from National Steel. This was my first real business deal, something that I had started from scratch and successfully concluded, very profitably, all by myself. The deal made me experience a high that I had never experienced before. This is the same high that I live for even today!

MY LEARNINGS

I believe that entrepreneurs must learn business development and sales skills early in their careers. Generating business needs passion and drive. The salient process of sales must be experienced first-hand by an entrepreneur, and not delegated to someone else. I believe that a market is available to anyone who has the persistence to keep knocking on doors and asking for business. The simple lesson I learned was that business begins to happen when you work towards activating it.

How Dare You Call Me 'Yaar'?

One of Mumbai's lucrative businesses is supplying drinking water to buildings through water tankers. The water is drawn from natural underground wells in and around the city.

In my early years at work, someone suggested to my Nana that he bid for the contract of supplying water to the Oil and Natural Gas Commision (ONGC), a Fortune 500 Company owned by the government of India. ONGC operated its oil and gas rigs off the Mumbai shore and they needed a constant supply of potable water. Without much thought, he bid for the contract and won it. (My Nana often took business decisions impulsively. Luckily for him, most worked out profitably.)

This one though was a disastrous decision. ONGC was a tough client and the unorganised private owners of the wells that supplied us the water were very unpredictable and unprofessional. We were squeezed from both sides. What added to the pain was that our tankers had to move in and out of the Mumbai docks since our ONGC delivery station was located at Victoria Docks inside the Mumbai docks. That involved dealing with the Mumbai Port Trust which was another tricky matter.

In the first few days after we began supplying water, I went along with one of my tankers to unload it at the ONGC station. At the delivery point, a strict-looking ONGC inspector with a thick moustache climbed on top of the tanker to check if our tanker was full. I can't remember what happened that had led to me to exclaim, 'Yaar, what are you looking for? We have a full tank.'

'Yaar' is a very casual and informal greeting exchanged between Indian youth. It is almost never used in a formal business relationship. So, when the Inspector heard me use that word, he was incensed. He began screaming and shouting and said, 'Who the hell do you think you are—you bloody water supplier—to call me "yaar"?'

So there I was, all of eighteen, trembling with fear about what I had done. I later explained my mistake and apologised to my Nana, but he just smiled and said, 'It doesn't matter.' To me, he is a living God and the best example I can think of, of someone who has perfected the art of forgiving and forgetting.

After that incident, that person made life incredibly difficult for my Nana and me. No amount of apologies seemed to make a difference to him. He would just not cooperate with us and doing business with ONGC became extremely difficult. This was the typical style of an Indian government officer who enjoyed taking businessmen to task by bullying them. Of course, I realised I had been wrong too, but I felt this man was taking the matter too far.

Internally, I was feeling wretched and told my mother about this incident in a passing conversation. What I didn't know was that my mother was friends with the Shashi Ruia family (of ESSAR fame) and that she was in touch with them. Shashi Ruia, the billionaire founder of the ESSAR business group in India had interests in oil, energy, and shipping.

Most of the ESSAR Offshore Supply Vessels (OSVs) were servicing ONGC rigs at that time, and ESSAR was one of ONGC's biggest offshore partners. The water we would unload at the ONGC receiving station was directly fed into ESSAR vessels docked at the station.

A few days later, my mother called me and said, 'Alok, I have spoken to my friend, and she has asked you to call Shashi Uncle and explain your problem to him. Be honest and ask him for advice.' I was very nervous but gathered up the courage to call up Mr Shashi Ruia and arrange to meet him in his massive, elegant office at Nariman Point. I was trembling when I explained to him what had happened.

Mr Shashi Ruia laughed for a long time after hearing my tale. He deeply empathised with me and was stunned by my business drive and enthusiasm. He then picked up his landline phone and said something to his operator in Tamil. I heard the name of my ONGC Inspector in that conversation, but was not sure what the context was. Later, I learned that the Ruia family had lived for a long time in Chennai and all of them spoke fluent Tamil.

A few minutes later, the phone rang. Mr Ruia picked up the receiver and said, 'Hello, Inspector saab?'

The voice on the other side replied, 'Yes, who is this?'

Mr Ruia said, 'This is Shashi Ruia of ESSAR.' I could hear the dead silence at the other end.

Then the voice said, 'Sir, what can I do for you? What made you call me?'

Mr Ruia then said, 'Arre yaar, I have this bacchha (kid) in front of me, and he tells me that you didn't like being called "yaar" by him and you are punishing him for his mistake. Please let him be, yaar.' Mr Ruia made it a point to call the inspector 'yaar' many times.

You can imagine what happened after that. The ONGC officer became reasonable with us and began to treat me well.

MY LEARNINGS

When I shared this story with friends and acquaintances, a few felt that I was flaunting my high-level connections and was nothing but a rude, spoilt brat, who had gotten away with his obnoxious behaviour. But, I don't think that's true. Personally, I was ashamed of my mistake. This incident impacted me profoundly and also taught me that while mistakes are made by the young, the mature should forgive. This is exactly how bullying happens in real life and this often causes hurt and long-term pain.

As adults, we must be cautious as to how we correct our children and young colleagues, so as to improve them without impairing them. After the incident, I made it a point to learn and imbibe business manners, etiquette and the essential rules of business engagement. The more significant lesson I learned was that the busiest, most successful people in the world are available to help others if approached. All that one has to do is ask! Entrepreneurs thrive best when they regularly connect with accomplished people who can mentor and guide them. There are mentors out there waiting for you to ask them for help.

Being a 'Banker', Selling Drums and 'Solver'

One of my most favourite places in Mumbai is the Mahalaxmi Race Course. It's breathtakingly beautiful and a delightful place for a walk or a run. I began jogging there since I was sixteen and have been a regular ever since. During the summers and winters, there are horse races at the Racecourse and walkers and runners have to patiently wait outside, under the giant trees for the races to be completed. The wait is a meditation in itself.

One such summer, when I was nineteen, I got talking to an elderly gentleman. He asked me what I did. I said I was a student. When I asked him about his profession, he said, 'I am a banker.'

'Wow!' was my immediate response.

He then asked, 'What's so "wow" about being a banker?'

'I wish I could be a banker,' I replied.

To my surprise, his reply was, 'Done deal. Come to my house tomorrow morning, and I will make you one.'

The gentleman in question was Mr Malhotra, a retired Standard Chartered Bank executive now living at Altamount Road (the lane behind my home). When I reached his home the next morning, he explained his business proposition to me. As a well-connected banker, he had access to finance at attractive rates from many banks. The money could be used for discounting bills and LCs (letters of credit). Mr Malhotra could obtain the best rates, but needed deals to take advantage of his relationships. (LCs and bill discounting are financial instruments in which corporates who are due to receive an assured sum of money from other corporates can instantly encash their debts for a small discount or fee from reputed banks.)

I contacted all my transport business clients and began offering them attractive LC discounting facilities. One of my top clients who instantly came on board was Jindal Iron and Steel whose office was located on Peddar Road, also very close by to where I lived. My new business now revolved around a holy triangle—my home, the Jindal office at Peddar Road and Mr Malhotra's home at Altamount Road.

In a few months, we had discounted about one and a half crore rupees worth of LCs! My earning was paltry (about ten thousand rupees), but I got a kick out of being involved in a finance and banking business without actually having been employed in that industry.

In hindsight, I see this as the early stirrings of my entrepreneurship. But after a while, I was restless again and was asking my friends in college if I could do 'some business' for them. Sanjay Sapre, a dear friend, came from the family that ran Henkel Chemicals, a large chemical company in India. One discussion led to another, and soon, I was sitting in Sanjay's office with his Purchase Manager. The manager wanted to procure 'leak-proof drums'. Another college friend, Rajesh Rathi and I took up the challenge and we met many drum suppliers in Mumbai. It was a tough and dreary job, being out in the open yards and dirty godowns speaking to men who I thought were very crude in their ways. Our efforts bore fruit eventually, and we found a reliable supplier who could help us supply the perfect leak-proof drums to Henkel. That adventure earned me lots more pocket money and gave me an entirely new experience—in trading.

In the mid '90s, one the most significant problems with the Initial Public Offerings (IPOs) of the Bombay Stock Exchange (BSE) was that while investors paid advance money to companies for subscription and allotment of shares, companies would 'sit' on that money for months without bothering to refund the excess money on time. There was no regulator at that time who stipulated how the application money was to be handled and the rules of refund. This was a loophole that let the companies which were floating IPOs earn free interest on investors' money without any punitive action. Investors would pull their hair out in frustration at what they had to do to get their money back, but the lure of getting a few shares at rock bottom prices made them repeat the cycle over and over again. The trick of getting a refund of the excess allotment money out was to relentlessly follow up with the 'registrars' (the service companies managing the IPO) and harass them endlessly to get them to refund the money. Each investor's case had to be pursued separately.

In most IPOs at that time, there was also an 'NRI' (Non-resident Indian) quota for share allotment. It occurred to me that if Indian investors had such a hard time getting their money back from these IPO companies, then the NRIs living abroad were probably utterly helpless!

With this target audience in mind, I launched a business called 'Solver'. I still remember the logo I had designed for this venture—it featured two hands in a handshake. My service was to help NRIs get their IPO refunds quickly and without pain!

I advertised my service in the *Gulf Times* (most NRI investors were from the Gulf region). In a few weeks, I received my first order along with an advance payment—to help an NRI extract a substantial refund from an IPO he had subscribed to. I relentlessly followed up with the registrar and managed to get his refund quickly, well before the others. I helped a few others too.

These mini-ventures helped me get a feel of entrepreneurship during my formative years as a student and young adult. I learned that business was about connecting the dots between opportunities and people. 'Dhandha' (business) could be found anywhere—be it under the trees of the racecourse or in the yards of rundown godowns. An entrepreneur could do anything, anywhere, as long as he had the will!

MY LEARNINGS

If you are a parent, don't discourage your children from trying their hand at a simple startup such as operating a YouTube channel or selling goods through social media channels. A small, harmless venture will give them many valuable, real-world insights about business.

If you are a young person interested in becoming an entrepreneur, do think about starting a simple service or enterprise that might help you understand the basics of doing business. Many millennials nowadays launch small online advertising, social media and app development services startups. By the time you graduate, you will learn something about most of the pitfalls of business without losing time or money. Whatever business you want to pursue, try and spot a real problem (like the IPO refund issue I identified) and build a solution around it. If your solution is scalable and affordable, it can become a great business that will not just make you wealthy, but also help many people too!

Lessons from Stock Trading

On the ground floor of the building I have lived in since the early '70s, there is a branch of the Punjab National Bank (PNB). They've been there ever since we moved in, and given the location of the branch, most of our building residents have an active banking relationship with the bank.

While visiting PNB for my Nana's transport business, I met a young PNB employee called Jayant Sethna. He liked to be called 'Jayant Bhai', and that's how I began addressing him. Jayant Bhai (JB) was a bank employee by profession, but a die-hard stock trader by passion. Whenever I met him, he would keep giving me 'tips' and information about stocks and why I should be buying the ones that he recommended. It turned out that his brother-in-law worked at Dalal and Broacha (one of the oldest brokerage houses on Dalal Street, Mumbai) and JB was their sub-broker.

Thanks to JB's influence, I took a fancy to 'stock trading'. All day even as I worked in my Nana's office, I would keep calling JB and trade in stocks through him. If you're wondering who financed me, it was my Nana of course! He never said 'no' to anything I proposed. While my Nana owned several stocks of his own, he never traded in them. He had invested in the IPOs of some of India's top companies when they had first listed and had never sold those shares. His reclusive, non-participative stance irritated me. I would always quiz my Nana on stock prices and deal ideas, but he wouldn't engage with me. I would look at his legacy portfolio and quiz him, 'Nana, how many shares do you have of Colgate Palmolive?' He would say 'Yaar, I've forgotten. I bought them to get discounts on toothpaste because that's what your Nani wanted ...' Answers like these would baffle me and throw me off-balance. It was only decades later when I read about Warren Buffett that I realised that my Nana was the Indian mirror of that great investor.

Since I didn't understand my Nana's 'buy, sit and forget' strategy, I went ahead and actively traded in over one hundred stocks and executed over three hundred deals over time. As you would have rightly guessed, I gained and lost money as most day traders do. At the end of each month, I would typically have earned nothing. The 'kick' to trade seemed to be the more significant motivation for me than the small profits or losses I would make.

As I dove deeper into the markets, I came across a profile of Vallabh Bhansali of ENAM Securities (a leading equity research firm) and the discipline of research he brought to the otherwise senseless methods of stock trading and selection. Vallabh and ENAM went on to make history in India. I was then studying Commerce in college and given my fondness for accounts, I took it upon myself to investigate one sizeable corporate entity thoroughly. As usual, I turned to one of my transport clients and selected Jindal Iron and Steel with whom I shared a very deep relationship. At Jindal, I managed to meet a few, very senior people, dove deep into their balance sheets and profit and loss accounts and prepared a twenty-five-page report on the company, complete with scientific recommendations on why I thought the script was a good buy. At that point in my young life, I was convinced that I had to pursue equity research as my long-term career!

On a blistering hot day in the May of 1992, the Harshad Mehta scam broke, and the stock markets crashed like never before. All my gains were wiped out, and the total value of my stocks became much lesser than the original capital I had invested in acquiring them. That month I learned an important lesson: active stock trading is for losers. Somehow though, my Nana's portfolio seemed unaffected. Perhaps, his ignorance about the stock market concealed a secret strategy after all.

Post the Harshad Mehta meltdown, I lost interest in the stock market. My Nana's portfolio performance made me understand that doing nothing was doing everything. Jayant Bhai kept pestering me to do trades, but I stopped responding. The prices of my 'hot stocks' had fallen so much that I felt miserable selling them.

Over the next couple of years, I got rid of all my shares to get away from the stress and heartburn of even owning them. I wanted to wipe the slate clean. Jayant Bhai felt terrible as he began to wind up all my stocks. One day, he called and said, 'Alok Bhai, I have an idea for you. We have little value left in your dead shares. I want to sell all your junk stock and buy shares of this newly listed company called HDFC Bank with the money we receive. I think it will rise as its parent HDFC has risen over the years, and at that time, we can quickly sell your HDFC Bank shares and try and recover some of your losses.'

At that time, I thought this was JB's classic 'from the frying pan into the fire' tactic. I had not heard of HDFC Bank, and it sounded as good or as bad as the other stocks JB had asked me to buy or sell. I was anyway fed up with the whole business of the stock market and told JB to go ahead and do as he pleased.

A few months later, JB disappeared. I have no clue where he went or where he is today. Someone told me he had moved to the US. In any case, with him gone, my share trading completely stopped. And there was no one to remind me that I owned HDFC Bank shares.

Almost a decade later, when the Securities and Exchange Board of India (SEBI) began to insist on all shares being dematerialised, I began consolidating my Nana's portfolio and discovered the HDFC Bank shares that Jayant Bhai had bought for me. The value of the shares at the current market price shocked me! It made up for all the losses I had suffered and more! I was ecstatic and told my Nana that I had accidentally emulated him by buying a good stock and then forgetting about it. My Nana gently smiled at me. I think he was happy that I had finally understood how wealth was created.

MY LEARNINGS

My crazy stock trading days and the losses I suffered instilled a profound learning and realisation in me that there is no 'easy money' in this world. If it comes easy, it will go away even easier. My stock analysis of Jindal Iron and Steel taught me that it takes a vast amount of time, patience and application to understand a business and its operations. It hit me hard that if just analysing a company was so hard, running a real business operation would be 100x times harder!

My tryst with my HDFC Bank shares taught me that wealth gets created with patience and perseverance ... and some good luck!

And one more thing: strategically doing nothing is doing something too!

Quitting a 'Difficult' Business

At the time I began working in the transportation business of my Nana, the culture of the trucking and cargo industry in India wasn't a very honest one.

We owned only a few trucks of our own, and when we received bulk transportation orders from our clients, we would rent more trucks from the open market. These trucks were owned by many individuals who in effect became our subcontractors.

When cargo needs to be moved, it needs to be moved. Especially if it's sitting in the Mumbai docks, attracting 'demurrage'—a punitive fine imposed by the Port Authority when cargo is not moved within a stipulated time.

After receiving a bulk transport order, I would frantically call the truck owners we had in our database and request them to dispatch their trucks to our loading points. These owners would be very receptive on the phone and confirm that they were sending their vehicles after finalising their rate agreement with me. They would give me their truck numbers and promise me that their trucks would reach the designated place in a couple of hours or even less.

Over time, I learnt that there was no value to their promises. Very few of these people actually had idle trucks to dispatch. The truck numbers they would give me were all fictitious! When I would call them back to check what had happened to their vehicles, they would narrate the same stories again and again to me: 'The truck developed a tyre puncture'; 'The driver fell ill'; 'The truck suddenly broke down' etc.

None of these truck owners were honest. Based on their false confirmation, I would communicate to our clients that our transportation plan was in place and things were under control. Then the delay in picking up cargo would cause lots of bad blood and disputes between my customers and me. They would debit my firm with their financial losses incurred due to our inability to pick up their cargo on time.

This situation depressed me. At that time, I never understood ever why truck owners lied and made false promises, in the most convincing manner. Later, I learned that these petty operators would regularly trick and cheat customers till such time that they became desperate to move their cargo and agree to pay the unreasonable rates that these unscrupulous folks demanded. Since we were just another transport company to truck owners, they lied to put us in a difficult situation. Lying and cheating had become their modus operandi.

Alongside, I also learned that owning our own trucks was no guarantee to things becoming smooth either. The drivers we hired were illiterate, stubborn and bent on making extra money on the side to supplement their income. Ever so often, we would get phone calls from our drivers from different parts of the country telling us the strangest stories to extract money. The drivers would say that the truck had broken down; been impounded by the police; had burst its tyres and all kinds of sordid tales. One driver called and said, 'Sir, the battery of our truck has fallen off. I will drive it to the nearest petrol station and then get a new one installed with my own money. You will need to pay me when I come back to the office.'

After a few seconds of silence, I asked him, 'How can you drive the truck without a battery?'

There was no answer. The illiterate man had no clue that a truck needed a charged, connected battery to be driven.

By the time I was close to finishing college, I had decided that I did not want to be associated with the transport business. I explained my decision to my Nana and told him, 'Nana, I cannot sleep night after night knowing that I have a bunch of liars and thugs as my business associates and employees. Very soon I will become like them.'

My Nana said, 'I am so happy you have discovered a higher ground for yourself. Your Nani and I had never planned to let you continue in this business even if you wanted to. This was just for your grounding and training.'

I was relieved and grateful to have such amazing grandparents who did everything they could within their power to make me shine and grow.

MY LEARNINGS

The lessons I learned operating my Nana's transport company have remained with me forever. I determined that any business associate or a person inherently deceitful or untruthful is not worth being involved with at all. If you get used to cheating and manipulating people and businesses for quick, selfish gains, it quickly becomes your nature. All through the years, my choice of not participating in anything that seemed unfair or tricky (internet-based gambling games, for instance) has deprived me of serious profits, but when I reflect on my decisions, I have no regrets. I have realised that by pursuing pure, unadulterated businesses, an entrepreneur can get the best out of himself and his team and the goal of the enterprise then becomes the search for excellence, not the management of lies.

'Learn to Sit'

I began working at my father's socks factory, Hindustan Hosiery Industries, the day after my last exam at college. The factory was located in the heart of the mills area in South Mumbai and comprised of many large 'galas' (halls).

On my first day, as I walked through the factory to acquaint myself with the business, I was stunned by the number of people working there and the massive bales of yarn that were piled up neatly against the walls. I remember loudly exclaiming, 'We employ so many people and use so much yarn, so why aren't we exporting our socks?' My Dad chose not to reply. His company did not export a single pair of socks, despite India being a big garment exporter at that time. My Dad had a mental block towards exports. He felt it involved too much risk vis-à-vis the rewards it may have earned.

When I entered my Dad's wood-panelled cabin, I proceeded to sit opposite him, on a somewhat comfortable chair. My Dad signalled to me to get up and sit on another chair that seemed rather creaky, stiff and small.

He said, 'Alok, for the next few days and months, you will have to learn to sit in that chair.' I was stunned by his remark. My Nana with whom I had worked earlier was an easygoing person, without any hard and fast rules. It was my first day and already, my new job with my father seemed to be a tough one.

So, I began to 'sit' day after day, week after week on that small chair absorbing everything that happened in my father's cabin. When I felt stifled, I would go for a tour of the factory. Socks are knit on small diameter circular machines, and my father's company had over five hundred of them, operated by three hundred people, over three working shifts. The machines produced a variety of children's, ladies', and men's socks and each socks machine was fed a dizzying range of cotton, polyester, acrylic and nylon yarn that changed as per the product being manufactured at that time.

To try and remember this puzzle, I began writing down each machine's specification, the type of socks it made and the different yarns it consumed. For months I would get baffled, but soon, the pieces of the jigsaw began to come together. About a year later, I knew everything that moved on the factory floor. One day, in a shop-floor meeting, the head technician complained that he did not have the spare parts for a machine that had broken down. With some trepidation, I quietly mentioned that a machine of similar specification was lying unused in the far corner of the hall. I was right!

That was my first victory in the factory. All the shop-floor managers looked at me and smiled, while my father nodded in acknowledgment.

Back in the cabin, I learned some crucial lessons in business. My father was very detailed and meticulous and would often conduct short but powerful meetings with his managers. I learnt how outstanding payments were tracked on a day-to-day basis; the manner in which dealers and distributors were dealt with when they didn't perform or meet their targets and many other things. Every day there was some problem or the other with regard to the workers and I learned how my father's factory manager deftly handled them. To this date, I believe that some of the most critical lessons of my life were learnt in my father's cabin. When things got a little boring I would look at my father's sales guy who had this habit of tucking one pencil behind his ear while taking notes with another pencil. The pencil behind the ear would get used and would grow smaller and smaller, but he would still manage to keep it neatly lodged there!

A very touching event would take place every other month. I would spot a very old worker sitting next to the factory cashier along with a couple of his relatives. When the opportunity came, the worker would gently knock on my father's cabin door, enter nimbly, gently walk towards my father and then bend down to try and touch his feet. The first time this happened I was stunned. It was very demeaning to see such a senior man behaving in such a subservient way. My Dad immediately stopped the man from bending further, did a 'Namaste' and greeted the man. I noticed tears in the old worker's eyes. I learned later that workers like him had worked for years in our factory and that was the day they had withdrawn their Provident Fund balance saved through their service in the factory over many years. The workers needed this money for personal events like their daughter's wedding or for buying a home. The amount these workers received when they withdrew their provident fund accounts were largely disproportionate to their monthly salary (lakhs of rupees compared to a few thousand). It would be a pleasant surprise for them. Workers completely relied on the company to safeguard a significant part of their life's savings, and considered these monies securely banked with us for an important occasion.

From their smiles after collecting their cash, I realised that they had worked all their life for this special day!

After three years of sitting, learning, observing, and contributing, I was allowed my very own, small little office. I chose to locate my office in the largest production hall because I felt closest to the socks machines there and loved the sound of their humming. Finally, I had graduated in the 'art of sitting' and had earned the right to sit separately.

MY LEARNINGS

Sitting quietly taught me the value of patience and the power of observation. I realised how important it was to inculcate the discipline of self-learning to become adept at business and develop an expertise. I realised that while books, schools, teachers and professors do teach you many things, learning does not end when your stint in an educational institution ends.

There is an inexhaustible reservoir of lifelong lessons a person can imbibe by just being aware, and by asking the eternal questions of why, when, what, who and where, as often as possible. This is the framework I adopted to learn everything about my father's factory. My interaction with the workers exposed me to the importance of ethics, values and responsibility and also how it was critical to be able to live up to the trust that people so often blindly placed in us.

How Much Does This Sock Cost?

I studied accounting in school and later, it was my major in college as well. My first job in my Nana's transport company was to review the books of accounts to discover errors and omissions by the managers (I never found any!). I liked financial numbers and the accountability they promised.

In the socks factory, I asked my father about the costing of the socks we produced and their pricing formulae. I was shocked when he told me that he did not know. My father mentioned that one of his brothers had created a price list for the company many years ago and that price list was increased in an ad-hoc manner each year, around Diwali. When new styles of socks were introduced, they were either matched with the price of the products of our competitors or were based on prices of similar products of the company. There was no detailed, granular costing of each type of socks manufactured in the factory. Hence, there was no clarity on the profitability per stock keeping unit (SKU) that we sold. I took it upon myself to create a detailed costing of every product manufactured by the factory.

I began by manually weighing different yarn cones before and after they were fed into the sock machines to calculate the exact quantity of yarn used per unit of socks. I created a special 'electrical meter' to measure how much electricity was consumed by different machines in the factory, to calculate their energy costs. I separated labour costs, packaging, and other overheads and allocated them to each style of socks that we sold. It took me three long years to create the most detailed costing of a socks factory that I believe has ever been created in the world. At the end of it, I knew every paisa that went into every sock and could even allocate the cost of coffee consumed by the directors per unit of socks! To date, this remains one of my most significant achievements.

The application of this knowledge was profound. My Dad was aghast to learn that his best-selling products were yielding very low margins, while some were even selling at a loss. I deduced that this was the precise reason those products sold well. They were cheaply priced as compared to the quality they offered. Consumers were the smartest people in the world and snapped up quality when they spotted it. This costing also revealed the actual Return on investment (ROI) on each of the sock machines we owned. An entire line of Czechoslovakian equipment imported over two decades ago by the factory was loss-making. On the Diwali of that year, my father re-hauled the entire price list of the company. Prices of some items were increased by a whopping fifty to hundred percent. My father understood that it made no sense to sell individual sock products at a loss just because the factory made a profit overall. I believe that I instilled the discipline in the factory that each sock we made had to be profitable. Amazingly, the market took the price hike very well. After a few grumblings and complaints, our order books went back to their original levels. One dealer even called my Dad and said, 'We never understood how you sold those socks at such low prices.'

MY LEARNINGS

I learned the fine art of costing through this very intensive exercise. The hard work to calculate costs to their minutest levels and to then allocate them for each sock we manufactured made me adept at costing and therefore, at deciding the pricing of products. I firmly believe that every business must be broken down into the atomic details of its costs. The most critical metric entrepreneurs must know is the margin (profit) on what they sell, and that can only happen when they know their costs. I insist that entrepreneurs must understand their business costs as intimately as possible and not just rely on accountants to figure out or advise them. Costing is the lifeline of a business and must be appropriated, reviewed and actioned upon by the owner and founder directly.

I Spot a Rainbow!

Exactly a year into working in my Dad's socks factory, between the first and the third of July 1991, the then Finance Minister of India Dr Manmohan Singh officially devalued the Indian rupee by almost twenty percent.

This meant that it would become costlier for Indians to buy dollars and pounds. But on the other hand, it also meant that exporters would earn twenty per cent more for all the dollars and pounds they earned courtesy the goods they sold!

The first day I walked into my Dad's socks factory, I had exclaimed, 'We employ so many people and use so much yarn! Why aren't we exporting our socks?' The rupee devaluation made me intuitively realise that the time had come for me to try and develop an export strategy for the company.

Many readers may be taken aback when they hear that in 1991, there was no google.com available to do research! There was no organised method available to me to gather information about companies worldwide who imported socks. When I reflect on this, I realise that one of my most educative periods in business development was the time I spent trying to find global buyers for my socks. To identify potential buyers, I went to all the trade commission offices of most of the developed countries located in Mumbai to find the addresses of the most prominent fashion retailers in Europe and North America. I also went to the Garments Export Council in Mumbai and asked them for help. They had never heard of socks exports before. When nothing worked, I began to chase garment exporters my family knew, for connections and contacts.

My father's first cousin—Anil Kejriwal (whose father invented the famous Kejriwal Eggs sandwich served at cafes all over the world)—was by far the most helpful and supportive family member I met. Anil was one of the most reputed garment exporters of India at that time, and he began inviting me for meetings with his buyers who were not considering buying socks, but were intrigued to find out more about them.

Over the next two years, I met several buyers in hotel rooms, lobbies and coffee shops. Most of them had minimal requirements or wanted socks that we did not manufacture (such as mountaineering socks or woollen socks). While I was in the factory, I would write hundreds of letters and send thousands of faxes (email was still not in use) to potential sock buyers with the help of the database I had patiently collected from various sources. Despite the large numbers of people I wrote to, none of them reverted. This is when I first learned about the concept of the sales funnel and the typically poor conversion rates associated with it. Not being able to find a single socks buyer for almost two years was one of the most frustrating periods of my life.

One morning, Anil called me and said, 'Alok, come with me to C&A today. They have a new team, and I want you to meet them.' C&A was a famous high street retailer in Europe with flagship stores in most of the major cities. Their logo was a rainbow ribbon with C&A etched in the centre. I distinctly remember a massive store of theirs with its distinct logo visible from the Marble Arch in London.

C&A had large sourcing operations in India and operated

out of Andheri. Anil introduced me to the principal merchandisers there, who were intrigued by this new category of socks. They reviewed my range carefully and promised to get in touch.

Little did I realise at that time that Anil had introduced me to one of the best partners I would ever have in my life. C&A would soon become our largest client and remain so for years to come. For that, I am eternally grateful to Anil.

MY LEARNINGS

I believe that for an entrepreneur, awareness of macro and micro business matters is very critical. Entrepreneurs must always have their ears on the ground, looking for signals and developments around them, to seize a business opportunity. With this very discipline, I spotted a chance in the devaluation of the rupee and acted upon it, even though this event had no direct correlation with my business.

While trying very hard to get my first business order, I learnt about the tough grind of business development. A lot of backbreaking work, patience and persistence is required when you are trying to sell something. You can multiply that effort many times when you are trying to sell something that has never been sold before. A successful sale can sometimes even take years and frustrate the most optimistic of sellers. Having infinite patience to sell is a critical lesson for startup entrepreneurs.

Red, Black, and Navy

An extremely driven and motivated lady called Olivia and her assistant Gayatri were my contact persons at C&A in India. I had met them several times and pitched my entire socks range for exports to their stores. All I could do was to wait for them to revert.

One afternoon, I received a call from Olivia. She asked me to come to the C&A Andheri office the next day for a meeting with a potential buyer. My heart began to beat fast!

The next morning, in the C&A office, I was introduced to the tallest man I've ever met. He worked for Marca Trading, an affiliate of the C&A group with a majority of their stores based in the Netherlands. I tried to start the conversation with pleasantries and small talk, but the Dutchman Mr. Mortelman cut to the chase and said, 'I want 12-24 socks in red, navy and black cotton, four pair bundles. What is your price per pack, in guilders?

It took me a few seconds to absorb what he said and that's when I realised that I had no clue what he was asking for.

Olivia and Gayatri came to my rescue and suggested I return to my factory and send a quotation. While I was exiting the C&A office building, Gayatri caught up with me and explained that the buyer wanted baby socks (for babies aged between twelve and twenty-four months which was what he had meant when he said 12-24) in solid cotton colours, packed in bundles of four. I was very excited! This was probably going to be my first export order.

Back at the factory, my father and his factory team were

neither impressed by my achievement of securing the first export order for the company nor convinced that we could manage to supply this small, simple order. At this point, it might be a good idea to bring into the story what my father's managers were like. Firstly, they always agreed with what my Dad said and never had a contrarian point of view. Secondly, they never wanted to do anything different from what they had been doing for the past twenty years. Every new idea presented to them received one standard response—an emphatic 'No'.

While evaluating the order I had secured, I heard them passing comments such as, 'We have never made such small socks. How will we do it now?', 'Where are the pressing farmas (aluminum cut outs on which socks are boarded to be pressed by machines) for ironing these socks?', 'The red colour ordered will bleed', etc. What crushed me most was a remark the head of the production department made with a grave face. He said, 'This business will be a total loss.' Amidst this swirling storm of negativity, I stayed positive, did not relent and kept pushing for the acceptance of my order. The value of the goods that I had to supply was a fraction of the company's total revenues, and I also had my costing calculations to prove that this export sale would be very profitable if executed correctly and on time. My father, exhausted by my ceaseless persuasions finally relented.

'Okay, go ahead,' he finally said.

The very next day, I submitted my bid and was given an official order by the buyer. Once I received the green signal, I began manufacture of the socks at the factory under my direct supervision. My office on the production floor became my operations center for the next seven years. While executing this particular order, I learned how treacherous the colour red was. All the Indian yarns that matched the red swatch (colour sample) supplied by my buyer bled colour. It took me many trials to get the red colour right! In the factory, no one knew the foot size of European babies between the ages of one and two. I begged C&A to source baby sock mannequins for me, so that we could get their sizes right.

When I look back now, I must have done many new and different things in the factory, things that had never been done before. All that just to complete an order so small that it would have passed unnoticed in the factory, if not for the experiments that had to be conducted to make it happen. But deep inside, I sensed that I was onto something big.

I executed my order a week before its deadline and it passed Quality Control without an issue. Almost two years after joining my father's factory, I had finally done something on my own.

MY LEARNINGS

This experience of securing and shipping my first export order taught me the hard tenets of entrepreneurship. I learned to persist at things even when people thought they couldn't be done; to be tenacious and to persevere while chasing an outcome; to be able to source, invent, research, manage and optimise resources and people. I learned not to feel let down by negativity, naysayers, and disbelievers. A thumb rule I came up with through this experience is that a startup entrepreneur will need to do at least 'x' number of unique things never done before by him or the world, before succeeding in his/her startup. That x number is his/her age when he/she starts up. I was twenty-four years old when I completed my first socks export order (never done before in the company or country), and I know that I reinvented or changed at least twenty-four different things to succeed in executing this order. To this day, I still believe that my first export order remains one of my life's biggest wins.

Being Truthful Is Being Profitable!

One incident made a profound impact on me when I was working at my father's factory. I had received a large order of 'Argyle' socks (the typical diamond pattern with the crisscross lines that you often see on sweaters) for export to a famous high street retailer in Europe. This was my first order for this particular style of socks. The Argyle patterns my buyer had ordered were complicated to produce because of the multiple colour combinations of the diamonds and their unique crisscross stitch lines.

Once the production was complete, we packed the socks in three-pair colour combination bundles. The socks were wrapped together using adhesive stickers that displayed the size, price, and other details of the socks. Everything was ready.

I then casually picked up a bundle that lay on my desk and opened it just like a consumer would, after buying it from a store. As I ripped the adhesive sticker from the socks, my heart stopped beating. The yarn threads of the small crisscross lines that ran through the Argyle diamond pattern began unravelling too! A brand-new pair now looked like an old pair with the threads dangling. The threads had gotten affixed to the strong adhesive of the sticker and were not strong enough to stay embedded in the sock. This meant that the top sock in every sock bundle would be damaged when a consumer opened it.

I froze. This wasn't looking good. I had no clue what to do next. It was one p.m. The shipment was to leave my factory for the docks in the next three hours. The socks had passed inspection by the buyers' quality team and were marked as good to go. (I assumed that the quality team had either not opened the bundles of the socks or that the adhesive on the sticker had become problematic over time). Technically speaking, nothing could stop me from shipping the order.

I still remember sitting quietly in my cabin, mentally arguing with myself and trying to decide between being 'correct' or being 'honest'. Never had I mentally duelled with these similar-sounding virtues before! I finally made my decision and decided to be honest. After taking a few deep breaths, I called the buyer. The buyer was surprised to hear from me and patiently listened without interrupting me as I described the problem to him. He had a sample socks bundle on his desk and replicated what I had done. The problem as I had detailed it for him was now clear.

The conversation that followed taught me one of the most significant lessons of all time. My buyer first thanked me for being honest and truthful. Then he shared that the Argyle socks supplied by other manufacturers in other parts of the world were also being returned by customers to their stores for the same reason. My buyer realised that the adhesive of the stickers supplied by his company was defective and that was causing the damage. He needed to find an adhesive that did not damage the sock. Then, he extended the delivery timeline without penalty and even paid for the extra top socks we had to produce! His company gave us many more orders in the years that followed and his quality team sometimes even skipped inspecting our socks before shipment. Clearly, we inspired a lot of trust now.

MY LEARNINGS

I realised very early in my career that there could be no compromise with honesty. Being correct was not even half as good as being truthful. I learned that respect and trust are won by being frank and honest. And when you have trust, respect and belief, there is no looking back at anything you do. I would urge everyone reading this to never compromise on morals and ethics, no matter what the situation may be. If you are confused, your conscience will always point you to the correct decision. Just be conscientious, and the rest will happen for the best.

Another critical lesson I learned from this incident is that partners, clients, associates, indeed whoever trusts you, always expect you to be entirely transparent and forthcoming about business matters, no matter how costly, ruinous or heartbreaking the information may be. Keep them informed and never feel hesitant in updating them about adverse developments. Bad times never last. Honest people always do.

The Business of Babies

As our socks export business began to scale up, I began visiting large retail stores in Europe to study their best-selling products, learn their presentation methods and investigate the sale prices of the different varieties of socks they stocked.

One of our most significant exports were of men's black socks, sold to H&M in packs of five pairs, in EU Size 9. Each five pair bundle cost me 1.50 Deutsche Marks (DM) to produce. I sold the same pack to H&M for 1.99 DM, netting me a thirty-odd percent profit on my costs. H&M, in turn, sold my pack for 4.99 DM to their consumers, earning almost a hundred and fifty percent margin on their cost, or five times more profit than what I earned! I understood that this is how high street retail operated and large operators like H&M had many costs and overheads that demanded such high markups. While I never grudged their massive profit margins, I was keen to figure out how I could improve mine.

One day in the H&M London store, while I was browsing in the men's socks section, I accidentally bumped into a lady shopper. Her shopping basket tumbled open, and I hurriedly began helping her put her merchandise back into the basket. While I was doing this, I noticed that she had bought a large collection of children's socks. What made my heart race was the price of those tiny bundles! They were priced at 4.99 DM—the same price as the men's socks! Like a thunderbolt, it dawned on me that when women purchased socks for their kids and husbands, they did not think too much about their prices. They were comfortable buying socks for their babies and their husbands at the same price. For them, at an emotional level, it probably meant the same thing.

When I returned to the factory, I talked about what I had observed to my father and recommended that we ramp up equipment to make baby socks. He wasn't convinced, but went with my suggestion anyway. We bought new sets of baby socks machines dedicated to our export business. A few months later, after many trials and samplings, I managed to produce a range of baby socks to present to my H&M buyer. After placing them flat on the table and looking at them, I had an inspiration and stuffed each of the tiny socks with butter-paper. The socks stood upright and looked very cute, all of them standing in a row!

When my buyer entered the room, he immediately noticed the socks and broke into a smile.

He asked, 'How much?'

'1.50 DM for two-pair packs,' I gently replied.

'Good! Let's start with 10,000 packs?' said he.

The baby socks packs I had sampled cost me 0.50 DM to produce because they were tiny and contained only two pairs in a bundle as compared to the five-pair bundle which was the standard for men's socks. Despite the significant reduction in my costs, I had still managed to sell the tiny socks at the 1.50 DM—the same price as the men's socks. Using simple observation and insight, I had increased my profit margins by an additional two hundred percent!

Baby socks also taught me another invaluable lesson in risk management. After receiving my first order for baby socks, I went to the H&M office for a special quality briefing with their European Director in charge of Quality Control for baby products.

The tall, blond gentleman greeted me and asked, 'Alok, congratulations on your order. Now tell me, what do you think babies will do with your socks'?

I was very puzzled and replied, 'Sir, I have no idea. Please tell me.'

He replied, 'Babies will put your socks in their mouths because that's what babies like to do with everything they find. After they do that, your socks could run colour inside the baby's mouth. If that happens, the mother will notice, get worried, then angrily storm into our stores and threaten to sue us. To prevent all this from happening, we need to make sure that the socks that you supply for babies are completely safe and bleed-proof.'

I gasped at what I had heard and fumbled for a suitable reply.

The blond gentleman said, 'Don't worry about how to handle this. We have recreated special synthetic, artificial baby saliva that you can collect from our office to use to test your socks. It replicates real baby saliva. If your products pass these tests, you will be all set to sell to us!'

The next day, we collected vials of 'baby saliva' from the C&A office and ran tests on our baby socks using it. We had to work on our red colour for a bit as it bled when left immersed in the saliva for a while. (Remember, babies don't take things out of their mouths once they put it inside.) After a few trials, we had perfected the red and the socks were good to ship!

MY LEARNINGS

My success with baby socks taught me that an entrepreneur must constantly do things to improve his margins in business. I learned how simple, yet accurate observations of the marketplace could be leveraged to improve business profitability. I realised that understanding my client's margins was as crucial as knowing my own. Constantly visiting retail stores gave me the opportunity to observe consumer psychology and this played a vital role in our product development process. Making my baby socks 'stand up' taught me the importance of presentation and packaging that went beyond just making great products.

'Seeing is believing and believing is buying' became my sales rule. Often, lots of people in the world make high-quality goods, but it's the superior marketeer and presenter who bags the order.

Also, the conversation about baby saliva taught me the concept of in-depth risk forecasting and the importance of coming up with strategies to mitigate those risks. The Director of Quality Control taught me how 'worrying' about business risk was a job in itself!

Being Overconfident

My first order of red, black and navy socks for children from Marca Trading was the starting point of one of the most successful business runs I've ever had in my professional life. Orders began to pour in from C&A and very soon, I was also working with the German retail giant Karstadt and with the Swedish giant H&M (not so well-known at that time). At the end of the first year of exports, the business that I had grown from scratch contributed to over ten per cent of our company turnover. By the end of the third year, it had reached seventy percent. The margins on my exports business were phenomenal because we were a specialised supplier from India, had no competition, and supplied to the top retailers in the world. It felt like heaven! With the benefit of hindsight, I think I can now say that my super-fast success led me to becoming overconfident.

One bright sunny Mumbai morning, I met a socks buyer from C&A in my factory showroom, and we began discussing new orders. The buyer winked at me, retrieved a bundle of socks from his bag and laid them on the table. The yarn colour and texture of the socks caught me by surprise. They looked like a combination of a heather mixture and grey flannel.

My buyer said 'Alok, this new yarn style is a rage in Europe. I am happy to give you an order five times larger than our regular order size if you can ship your socks in this new yarn and colour.'

When I asked him what the yarn was, he very casually replied, 'Oh, it's a cotton mélange. All the global socks manufacturers are working with this new yarn in their countries. I'm sure you will find suppliers for it in India, without a problem.'

I looked at him, then stared at the socks for a few seconds and without thinking further said, 'Yeah, I'll do it.'

Little did I realise that I had taken the greatest business risk of my life. Greed had blinded me. I should have ideally asked for time to undertake a trial order before committing to one that was five times the usual size.

Once I received the order, I began scouting the Indian market for mélange yarn that was suitable for socks knitting. None of my regular suppliers made that type of yarn. A few suppliers in Hyderabad were large producers of mélange, but their yarn composition was synthetic and not cotton. My export order required cotton yarn to be used. My sourcing problem was further compounded because I had accepted the orders in five distinct colours of yarns, not the usual 'grey mélange'.

I began to panic because I couldn't find a single yarn supplier of mélange yarn suitable for socks, in India. What haunted me was the non-fulfillment of the order for C&A—my biggest buyer who was responsible for more than eighty per cent of my export business! If I failed to deliver this order, I would be blacklisted for life. This order was beginning to look like a train wreck. After an agonising search and hunt operation, a Hyderabad based company—Suryavanshi Cotton Spinning Mills agreed to spin a special cotton yarn for me in their regular 2/40's count. (In cotton, the larger the count number, the finer is the yarn. 'S' stands for single yarn. 40's is good for knitted garments; 200's is what is used in shirts). I wanted 20's (20 single) which is typically used for coarse socks. 2/40 meant that two yarns of 40's would be twisted together to make it as thick as 20's (which is what I wanted), but the cost would be double of what I had estimated to pay for the 20's yarn. So buying 2/40's was a no-go. Somehow, I convinced Suryavanshi Cotton to spin the yarn in 20's (20 single counts).

When I received my yarn supplies and knit a few sample pairs of socks, I got a big shock. The socks knit with this yarn were 'twisting' and 'turning' as if they had been 'wrung' to death. This was because the socks were knit using a single thread (the 20's). If I had bought the 2/40's yarn, the socks would not have this problem because an 'S' twist and a 'Y' twist of each of the 40s yarn spun together would give the resulting yarn a 'neutral' spin. But as I explained earlier, I could not afford that yarn!

When I explained my agony to the mill, they asked me to 'heat' the yarn through a specific process to 'kill' the spin. I did just that and then came the second major shock—the colour of all the five yarns dramatically changed when 'heated.' After a torturous back and forth, I got a 'muted' version of the 20's custom cotton yarn made in five shades; then got that yarn heated to kill the twist while making sure that the resulting colours matched the original colour ordered. To remove any residual spin, I decided to wash the socks. Washing led to the shrinking of the socks (by then, I had become immune to shocks) and so I had to redesign my socks specifications all over again to make sure that after they were washed and shrunk, the socks perfectly matched the original size and colours that the buyer had ordered!

The entire process was the most prolonged, most frightening business nightmare I've ever lived through. I made my shipment on the last day of delivery with just a couple of hours to spare. All I know is that the universe conspired to make me successful.

MY LEARNINGS

You probably did not understand some of the technical problems that I have detailed in this chapter. It doesn't matter. But, I am sure you understood the agony I went through. Suffice to say, this horribly scary episode taught me some critical lessons. I learned that being overconfident is the best way to self-destruct. Also, I painfully realised that a single act of greed could kill a super-successful business. In the life of an entrepreneur, many opportunities present themselves, and each one must be evaluated meticulously before being accepted or rejected. I learned there is no need to say 'yes' on the spot in any situation, be it business or personal.

On the positive side, my relentless pursuit to accomplish what I had set out to achieve, my ability to motivate my partners to collaborate with me and my willpower to keep re-calibrating processes till I got it right taught me that anything was possible if one had the will and the intent. This incident unleashed the power of supreme belief and a sense of deep accomplishment in me. Entrepreneurs must go through such trying times to discover how strong they are!

You're a Liar—I: You Don't Know Your Machines!

I've been called a liar twice on my face in my professional life. Both events have proved to be auspicious inflection points, leading to remarkable improvements in my career.

The first time this happened was when I was on a trip to Europe as an enthusiastic socks exporter who had just begun exporting socks to famous retailers such as C&A and H&M. On a flight from London to Milan, I sat next to a middle-aged lady who asked me my purpose of travelling to Milan. I told her I was a socks manufacturer from India and planned to visit socks factories in Italy. She raised her eyebrows and immediately began asking me many questions in one go such as, 'What gauge of needles do your men's socks get knit on, how does your double cylinder machine make jacquard designs, what revolutions per minute does your single cylinder machines spin at ...' and so on.

I was dumbfounded. While I knew the basics of all my machines, my yarns, and counts, I had no clue what happened inside socks machines. I calmly replied, 'I don't know. We have mechanics and jobbers who know these things, and they take care of the technical issues.'

The lady sneered and said, 'You are a liar. No owner who operates a factory of the size and scale you mentioned is unaware of such technical questions. Owners know everything about their knitwear business, especially the nitty-gritties that makes things happen.' After reprimanding me, she began leafing through a book and did not speak to me again for the rest of the flight.

I was shattered and vowed to myself that I would learn everything about the workings of my machines and become a technical expert at my business. Later in the same trip, I discovered that most hosiery entrepreneurs in Europe were trained engineers and mechanics who knew their machines inside out. They worked on the shop floor with their workers, and technicians and their in-depth technical knowledge also helped them innovate new products.

The day I was back in Mumbai, I debriefed my Dad about my trip, the machines I had inspected and my recommendations. He liked my ideas and accepted my proposal to buy a brand new type of computerised Italian socks knitting machines whose sports socks were becoming very popular in Europe. Even as I was delighted at the acceptance of my proposal, I did not forget to say, 'Only on one condition. I will go to Italy myself, get trained on the machines, learn to build, repair and maintain them and operate them myself.'

My father was aghast at what I wanted to do and said, 'You want to become a jobber? A mechanic?'

'Yes,' I replied. 'It is something I should have done a long time ago.'

My Dad reluctantly agreed, and a few weeks later I was booked on a flight to Florence to buy a brand new computerised socks knitting machine which I was also going to be trained on to operate and repair.

Two of the three uncles I met heard about my travel plans and scornfully said, 'Oh, why are you becoming a mechanic? It looks so bad. What will people say?' I was very upset with their condescending attitude and headed straight for the airport. Little did I know what destiny had in store for me and how my life was about to change forever.

MY LEARNINGS

Being called a liar by the lady was probably a very good thing. The insult inspired me to overcome my mindset and forced me to stretch my capabilities and add to my knowledge. The incident taught me to rise above insults and instead use the occasion to introspect and to take action. When my relatives were making fun of me, I realised that some mindsets could perhaps never change. But as a businessman who sought to grow his business, I had to learn to ignore such people. I realised that all I needed to do was to follow my heart and do everything in my capacity to get better at my business and trade.

(P.S: If you are the lady who sat next to me and are reading this, please accept my profuse thanks and gratitude for calling me a liar. You changed my life and how!)

My Eureka Moment

It was July 1995. My hometown, Mumbai was awash in the monsoon. But there I was, on my way to buy a 'Conti Florentia' socks knitting machine from Florence, Italy. This machine had become very famous in the world because of the speed at which it produced sports socks (with a 'fake' heel, while ensuring consumer comfort). Each Conti machine cost twenty times the cost of a normal Indian socks machine. Buying this machine was a risky bet and it was something that I had proposed for our company. My agreement with my father was that I would personally be trained on the machine and get a thorough understanding of how it operated.

I still remember the first day of my training in the Conti factory at Florence. It was a warm July day, and the soft rays of sunlight were streaming from the skylight above. I felt so inspired! Florence was the epicentre of the great Renaissance movement, a city of many accomplished artists, and I felt fortunate to be in a holy, blessed place. My trainer at the Conti factory was a gentle, middle-aged man called Mauro Cecconi, and he started my training by making a very profound statement. He said, 'Mr Alok, there is no better way to understand a machine than to make one yourself! Let's start making the machine you have come here to buy.' Screw by screw, block by block, Mauro and I began assembling the machine I had ordered.

On the first day, after a couple of hours had passed, Mauro caught me looking around the factory floor and asked, 'What do you want?' I said, 'I'm looking for a chair.' Mauro said, 'There are no chairs in this factory. Your legs are your chairs. Learn to stand on them.'

That day, when I returned to my hotel room, my legs were swollen. I had never stood on my feet for eight straight hours. Over the next few weeks, Mauro trained me thoroughly on the machine, and I became very well-aware of all its moving parts, and its electro-pneumatic functions. This was a state of the art Computer Aided Design (CAD), and Computer Aided Manufacturing (CAM) machine and I was fascinated by how designs drawn on a computer screen could turn into a full sock in a couple of minutes. This was my first brush with digital creativity, and I was fascinated by its potential.

Once the machine was built, I returned to India, very confident that I could operate it and troubleshoot any problem myself. Three months later, we received our machine, and I got it installed rapidly. Given its massive cost, each day lost meant an extra burden on the company. Quickly, we began production of our line of sports socks and everyone in the factory was amazed at this super machine and the speed at which it churned out socks!

On the fourth day, without warning, the machine stopped working. I was stunned. I went through my breakdown checklist line by line but could not spot what the trouble was. My father kept asking me what had gone wrong. I had no answer to give him. The worst part was that the machine had broken down on a Saturday and that meant that I could not contact Conti in Florence until the weekend was over. Not running the machine meant incurring massive losses.

As I inspected the machine again, I figured out that a large blue exhaust fan fitted at the rear end of the machine was not starting up. This fan provided suction, and because it wasn't starting, the machine refused to turn on. Even though I wasn't trained on this fan because it was not original equipment made by Conti, I disassembled it from the machine and scrutinised it. It had the branding of Siemens engraved on it along with its product name and version.

A few days earlier before this incident, after months of pleading with my Dad (and he with his brothers), I had got an MTNL (a government-owned telecom company) internet connection installed in the factory. This was the time when modems would make horrific screeching noises while getting connected and websites would take hours to browse.

To figure out the problem with my Conti machine, I looked up this Siemens suction fan on lycos.com—a search engine that was very popular then. The search results pointed me to the Siemens website. Inside the site, after patiently wading through many pages at agonisingly slow browsing speeds, I managed to reach the webpage of this specific fan. There was a section called 'Frequently Asked Questions' (FAQ) on that page. When I clicked on it, the second bullet point read 'If the fan stops without any particular reason, check for the washer inside. That may have been torn or it may have worn out.'

I rushed back to the shop floor, carefully opened up the fan, and saw its torn black washer. It looked like a normal rubber washer, and I got my chief jobber to go out and look for a similar washer from the nearby Parel market. He returned with a pack of washers that looked like the original. I carefully put the washer in, reassembled the fan, fitted it back unto the Conti machine and pressed the START button. The machine roared back to life!

The washer packet had cost forty rupees for a set of twenty washers. A two rupee washer had saved the day.

This was a big Eureka moment for me. This was the first time I came face to face with the power of the internet, its omnipotent strength as the storehouse of the world's information and its innate ability to find solutions to any problem that existed. Something shifted inside me that day. I knew that the internet was my true calling.

MY LEARNINGS

My success in reviving my machine made me sincerely appreciate the adage: God is in the details. I realised that if an entrepreneur had to succeed, he had to get into the microscopic details of everything. The forensic approach I adopted to revive my Conti machine made me appreciate the principle of 'dirtying my fingernails' to stay on top of my game. (My fingernails were always greasy in the years I worked in the socks factory). It was clear to me—without getting into the micro, there was no way I could manage the macro. The other big lesson I learned was to curate, cultivate and unleash curiosity and always to try and keep learning new things. My unquenched thirst for questioning led me to find out why my machine had stopped. I found out who the manufacturer of the fan was, looked up the internet to find a solution, found it and then implemented it, becoming a hero in the process. Curiosity had saved me from a big disaster. I would implore you to develop curiosity as a serious habit. It could become your passport to success.

You Are a Liar—II: Why I Stopped Wearing My Socks!

The socks export business that I had grown from scratch for the family socks business was booming. With my sales growing a hundred percent every year, my division that was just five years old was at par with the company's Indian business that had been built over twenty-five years. In the process of creating this business, I had gained deep technical skills and operating knowledge of socks knitting machines and this had empowered the company to invest in and import complicated machines and equipment from all over the world. As if fate had willed it, I was the right guy, in the right place, at the right time.

Or was I?

My father co-owned the company with his brothers, but unfortunately, my uncles did not like me much. I'm not sure if it was jealousy or if it was a false sense of competitiveness, but from the first day I began working at the factory, they made life miserable for me. Their operating rules for me meant that I could not draw a salary, sign letters, send faxes, confirm agreements, have my own visiting card or write cheques. I was effectively persona non grata in the factory. The work I did was executed in my father's name, and every document, fax, and correspondence I generated was photocopied and stored for my uncles' scrutiny.

I had heard that money makes the world go round, but even after my exports business began generating handsome tax-free profits for the company, there was no softening of my uncles' hardline attitude towards me. I continued to be treated unreasonably. Their hatred and coldness towards me only grew. It was a very eerie existence; I felt like I was a prisoner of destiny within the factory walls.

My exports and machines business would require me to travel extensively, and on one trip from Frankfurt to Mumbai, I nearly missed my flight. When I was back in the factory the next day, I told my father, 'I need an international credit card because I need to have access to money. If I had missed my flight the other day, I wouldn't have had food to eat, because my cash had run out.' My father instantly agreed and gave me the go-ahead to get a credit card for myself that could be used for emergencies. He said he would deal with my Uncles in the event they raised a stink.

In the late '90s, credit cards were still a luxury and thought to be a vanity asset. I had to call (yup, you read that right!) Citibank to get a credit card for myself.

The lady who answered my call understood my requirement and asked me a set of standard questions, as per her diligence process. She asked me a series of questions: 'What is your salary?', 'What is your designation?' 'What is your expense credit in the company' etc. For each of these questions, I gave a combination of responses that included 'I don't have a salary. I am working for my father's company but without any designation. I don't have an expense account, but there is no limit to what I can spend.'

The Citibank lady patiently heard me for a few minutes and then said, 'You're a liar. There is no way you can export crores worth of goods, travel the world, have such an important job and remain identity-less. You are trying to defraud us by requesting an international credit card.'

Her retort hit me very hard. Here I was, being called a liar inspite of all the excellent work I had done. I felt low and defeated. Just because of the joint family politics at play, all my efforts were suspect, and I had been called a fraud by a junior credit card officer at Citibank! Was this the life I was destined to live?

That moment, just after the Citibank call ended, something changed inside me. The idea of moving out took hold of me. Life henceforth would be very different, I realised.

That was the day I felt it was time to stop wearing my socks!

MY LEARNINGS

Each entrepreneur comes across a profound, personal moment of calling—when leaving behind the past and starting out and doing one's own thing seems to be the only logical way ahead. I would implore readers never to ignore that calling irrespective of how difficult or impossible the occasion appears. In those moments of utter despair, you need to have a firm resolve, and take a single step forward, with a prayer in your heart. The rest happens magically.

A Spiritual Hippie Makes a Prayer

I have forever been something of a spiritual and religious hippie. I had and still have (maybe, just a little bit!) this insatiable fetish to visit temples and places of worship and seek out gurus, babas, astrologers, soothsayers, face readers, and people of that ilk.

When I reflect on this, I realise that my religious and spiritual leanings were a result of my upbringing. My Nana's family came from Mathura, the land of Krishna. Our house in Mumbai always welcomed anyone who claimed to be a man of God. As I grew up, I met many sages, saints and spiritual men, some of whom made a profound impact on me. I was deeply drawn towards temples. The Mahalaxmi and Babulnath temples in Mumbai were my favourites, but none of them could match the deep longing I had, to keep visiting the Bankey Bihari Temple in Vrindavan, Mathura. I cannot even remember when I had visited that temple the first time. The dark, childlike deity of Krishna remained imprinted in my mind, and I would seek him out whenever I was in trouble or pain.

As my personal troubles in my father's socks factory began to mount, I became very restless. I longed for freedom and wished to break free of the joint family trap and become successful on my own. As I saw it, there was no chance of my official inclusion in the factory because of the hostility of my uncles who harboured a strange hatred towards me. Their view was that the second generation of the family members (basically me) had no right to have any official position in the company as long as the founding brothers had not yet relinquished their position. And I wasn't in the mood to wait for fifty years to be able to sign letters and write cheques using my name!

One winter's day, things became nasty. I needed to travel to Delhi to meet one of my socks buyers who was visiting the city. Since there was a fog build up in Delhi, I requested my father to allow me to travel the previous night and also allow me to stay a night at the Hyatt Regency hotel. I was meeting my buyers in that hotel the next day and so staying there the night before would ensure a mishap-free meeting. I thought that my proposal would seem very practical and responsible to the owners of a business who were earning crores of rupees a year, thanks to my sales efforts and export orders. My father asked his brothers to approve my plan as was customary in the company.

To my surprise and dismay, they both said 'No'. In their view, I could take a very early flight (maybe at 2 a.m. or 3 a.m.) to try to beat the fog, and still make the meeting. It did not matter to them that I would be groggy and not in my best form if I travelled so early. Their larger agenda was to constantly provoke me by disallowing small and petty requests just to prove their position and status in the company. On many occasions, one of my uncles would taunt me and say, 'Who are you?', 'Where will you go?' 'You are going to be here forever, knitting socks and operating trucks.'

When my father called me on the intercom and told me about their decision, I sighed and felt very suffocated. I needed to get some fresh air and stepped out of the production floor to head towards my father's office located in the other building.

I still remember that day, that afternoon, the exact place in between the two factory buildings when I paused for a few seconds and remembered Bankey Bihari of Vrindavan with a heavy heart. I prayed, 'Bihariji, please get me out of here. Give me a business of my own that requires no money; one that makes me use my brains; gets me to meet the best people in the world and please do all of this for me now.'

How sweet and goosebumpy it feels now to reflect on how Bihariji heard me and gifted me all those things that I had asked for ... almost instantly. The next few chapters in the book will unveil that story entirely.

MY LEARNINGS

As an entrepreneur, I have learned that we have to deal with toxic people and situations and develop the ability to tolerate them to get on with our lives. But there comes a time when you want to break free. I have realised that the intent to gain freedom is of paramount importance. Feeling sorry for yourself and living in self-pity are counter-productive. Even if you are a nonbeliever, I would say that do consider praying sincerely for freedom and super success. There are unseen and unknown forces in the universe that are waiting with bated breath to grant you your wish. You have to activate them.

Of course, you then have to act to make things happen.

Party-time!!

A close friend of mine from school, Anurag Kanoria was hosting one of his famous winter parties in his palatial bungalow at Worli Seaface in Mumbai and had invited me to it. As I mingled with friends, I met Gurinder 'Bobby' Singh—an old pal of mine with whom I had hung out a lot in school. Bobby was excited about his recent achievements and began talking to friends about his new business of creating 3D architectural walkthroughs for clients such as builders and architects. They were using his services to present their construction projects in an exciting, new way. I was spellbound by the work Bobby was doing. This was akin to the creative technology I had seen when I had travelled to Italy to be trained on computerised socks knitting machines. Bobby rekindled the spirit of creativity in me and inspired me to do something new.

A little later, another close school friend Manoj Agarwal came by to say hello. As we spoke about ideas and technology, I brought up the story of the fantastic sale of hotmail.com created by Sabeer Bhatia to Microsoft. Manoj said, 'Alok, believe it or not, Sabeer Bhatia studied with my sister in the US, and they have many common friends.'

I don't remember too much of the rest of the conversation. But I remember him saying this: 'Alok, someone like you and me created Hotmail ...'

That evening, I was all fired up. As the millennials of today would say, I was 'lit'. I intuitively knew that the internet could be the vehicle for my dreams. I had to leverage the internet that I had so fortuitously discovered while repairing my Conti machine. I had to do something creative and innovative. The internet was the escape hatch I was looking for.

The very next day onwards, I began to work on 'internet' ideas. My first website idea concept was balancesheets.com, and I booked that domain for myself. In the pre-internet era, Indian stock analysts relied on printed balance sheets to analyse the stocks they were interested in. Only shareholders received company balance sheets. If an analyst did not own a certain company's shares, he had to write to the company requesting for a balance sheets. Those balance sheets rarely arrived. Even if they did, they came too late for a quick analysis. My idea was to digitise and update all the balance sheets of India in one website to serve as a repository for stock analysts and enthusiasts. But when I thought deeper about the idea, I realised there was no 'entry barrier' to it. Anyone could do what I had thought of, and there would be no long-term value I would be creating.

My next idea was of a religious, spiritual website where citizens could get 'darshans' of their favourite deities and even order 'prasad'. I commissioned my Nana to list out all the famous places of worship in India. When I thought of the business deeply, I realised that the connectivity and bandwidth available in India was so poor then, it would take ages to get a glimpse of a web page to download and give a devotee the darshan of a favourite God or Goddess. I bowed my head to the Gods and gave up on that idea.

One lazy Sunday, sitting on a sofa in my living room, out of nowhere, an idea popped in my head to create an online site for contests. It was nothing short of divine intervention that inspired me to think of what would eventually become my site: contests2win.com. I was fond of participating in brand contests. I had always felt that they were clumsily managed in India. Contestants had to first buy competition postcards from the post office, respond to the contest questions on those postcards and finally post them to the 'P. O. Box No.___' of the sponsoring company. Very often, contestants like myself forgot the contest question asked, or the number of the 'P.O. Box'. I thought about this defective process deeply and asked myself, 'Why can't there be an online destination for contests that allows everyone to enter all the contests in India in one place, with one user ID, and avoid the hassle of cutting, pasting, posting and even forgetting to participate?'

Just by chance, I had hit upon the biggest idea of my life!

MY LEARNINGS

A critical lesson of this story for me is the importance and benefit of meeting people. By going to that party and mingling with friends, I found that spark of inspiration because of which I began to think in terms of starting an internet business. It's comfortable and convenient to skip events, meetings and boring parties and stay comfortably at home, but often, it's in those places that bright ideas germinate in your mind while interacting with people. I firmly believe that entrepreneurs and professionals must meet at least one new person daily in their lives. It does not matter what the agenda is or how the discussion pans out. I have met over seven thousand people so far and have learned something unique from every one of them!

Another valuable lesson I learned that while every idea of an entrepreneur is fascinating, it is also crucial to process each idea carefully and beat it down as hard as possible, to find potential flaws and defects. An entrepreneur must play devil's advocate to each of his plans to test their strength and viability. If the idea still wins, it's a green signal for the entrepreneur to go ahead.

The Sudden Appearance of My Guru—Gopala Krishna!

While the idea of an online contests website grew in my mind as being unique and useful, I did nothing about it. Or to be more honest, I could not do anything about it. I had no clue what creating a website meant, leave alone creating a very specific one with a business idea that had never been done before. I browsed the internet for other contests sites and found none. So all I did for some time was to keep baking the idea in my head.

At the factory, one early morning, I received a call from the telephone operator Mr Salvi on the intercom. Salvi had been working with my father for twenty years and had a distinctive character and style of his own. He said, 'Alok babu, there is the man called Gopala Krishna here to meet you. He says he wants to sell computers to us. He is very dark.' (This was Salvi's style. He often described a visitor's physical appearance on the phone, often in unflattering terms, sometimes within earshot of the visitor.)

I have come to realise that sometimes, luck and providence come directly to your doorstep and yet the untrained mind chooses to close the door on them. I told Salvi, 'Tell this guy to meet the IT team. I don't need to buy computers.' Salvi called back and said, 'Gopala says he wants to meet you only.' I was irritated, but reluctantly agreed and asked Salvi to send Gopala down to my cabin on the production floor.

The moment I met Gopala Krishna (GK), I knew he was different. His eyes twinkled when he spoke, and he had an enthusiasm that was very infectious. He said, 'Mr Kejriwal, I want to suggest that you make a website for your socks business. You can find global buyers for your amazing products that remain undiscovered in the world. Your website will help you connect these buyers with your company.'

I guess I was so daft that I still didn't get it. I did not connect the dots when Gopala spoke about the internet. I stupidly asked Gopala to send me a proposal and also attach a printed report of all the Yahoo! search results he could find of other socks businesses in the world.

A few days later, something shifted in me. There is a favourite Sanskrit shloka of mine taught to me by my spiritual guru Sri Sri Ravishankar that reads 'Satyam Param Dimahi'. It means 'May the transcendental truth dawn on your intellect.' All of a sudden, without any stimulus, it dawned on me that I could get GK to help me create my online contests website—not a website for our socks factory!

I called GK and excitedly said, 'GK, forget the socks website I had asked you to research. I have something new and amazing to discuss. When can we meet?' GK sensed the urgency in my voice and said, 'Mr Kejriwal, come over to my office. I am waiting for you. It's best if you see my set-up and we can then also discuss your plan.'

Fifteen odd years later, I managed to connect the dots: I had prayed to Bankey Bihari—the dark-complexioned Krishna to help me redeem my life. It was he who had sent to me the dark-complexioned Gopala Krishna.

GK was equally excited when he heard my contests website idea and asked me if I had a website design in mind for contests2win. I still remember how I began drawing all the pages and wireframe designs of the website on a white paper with a ballpoint pen, without making any significant corrections. It felt as if a higher power was directing my hand to draw the page designs. GK looked at the drawings, seemed very impressed and said, 'Sure, Mr Kejriwal. Why don't you come to my coding office on 14th Road, Khar (Mumbai) tomorrow morning and we will get your website started?'

I distinctly remember that day when I reached the cozy garage office in a building in Khar. GK and I sat in front of an old computer. He began talking about the software he was using and began assembling the website I had drawn out on paper for him. Over the next few days, GK taught me to code, create contests, web pages and run a simple database at the backend. While I was not a programmer, GK made it very easy for a novice like me to understand how my primary site operated.

Contests2win.com was soon up and running and open for business!

MY LEARNINGS

The most important lesson I learned was being proactive and initiating the execution of an idea. I've noticed that while many of us think of ideas, (some genuinely brilliant), very few of us do

something about them. We all procrastinate, delay
taking action and then painfully watch our great
ideas become someone else's successful business.
You have to get up, get out, do something and just
get started. Also, another learning is to leverage
the people you meet, to achieve your goals, in the
same way that I leveraged Gopala Krishna to
help me create my website. All you need to do is
connect the dots!

What Does Your Idea Have to Do with the Internet?

My internet guru Gopala Krishna (GK) had helped me bring to life my contests site—contests2win.com. Initially, the site hosted demo contests to present to brands and sponsors. A very kind relative—Vibha Khandelwal—lent me her precious laptop to help me demonstrate my site to potential sponsors. Laptops were quite rare those days, and having one, even for a little while, made me look smart.

Now that my site was up, all that I needed was content! Simply put, I needed real contests of real brands to go live on my website.

I was starting from ground zero. I had no background in advertising, marketing, branding or communication. I was a B Com graduate with a major in accounting. For seven long years before this internet idea had hit me, I had manufactured socks in a factory in Lower Parel. I had no clue about meeting brand managers and getting them to host their contests on my site!

I remembered how I had canvassed for new business deals for my Nana's transport business and garnered exports orders for my father's socks factory and decided to implement the same strategy and game plan that had worked for me. It involved creating a detailed list of all those brands that ran contests, meeting the brand managers personally and convincing them to partner me.

As I began to scour newspapers, magazines and television

channels, I was amazed at the high volume of contests that were being regularly promoted in India. This was proof of a developing market that tempted consumers with freebies and offers to prompt them to buy more and more products from the advertiser. I prepared lists of brands and companies and began calling them using the humongous three-volume thick Mumbai Telephone Directory. Remember, there was still no google.com back then!

On a typical day, I would make about fifteen to twenty telephone calls, but wouldn't get past the telephone operator. On a rare occasion, I would get connected to a junior brand executive who would speak to me reluctantly. Most of the time she or he would be in a hurry to get rid of me.

My inability to connect to the right people was entirely my fault. The minute someone picked up my call, I would ramble about my internet idea, without stating the purpose or benefit of my company and service. The person on the other end of the call would not understand what I was trying to say and would sometimes just disconnect the line. Take, for example, the umpteen number of calls I made to Britannia, one of India's top biscuit manufacturers. For about sixty-odd days, I called a number listed in the directory as one belonging to Britannia Industries Limited. The moment I would call, a rather unsophisticated man would answer and say, 'Hello, Britannia.'

'Boss, connect me to the Marketing Manager,' I would tell him. Imagine how vague that sounded. There was no context, no description of which marketing manager or brand team I wanted to speak to.

The man would reply, 'No. Call tomorrow.' I would then

obediently call the next day and hear the same message. One day, I assumed this person was fed up with me and broke out in Hindi. He then asked me what I wanted. When I explained my purpose to him, he informed me that I had been calling the storage godowns of Britannia Industries all this while! He was the godown watchman. The marketing teams of Britannia were all based in Bangalore!

One gloomy day, a manager in an advertising agency took pity on me and my helpless state and suggested that I focus all my energies in convincing Hindustan Lever Limited (HLL) to buy my internet idea. HLL was the Indian subsidiary of the global conglomerate Unilever. He said, 'Alok, if you can crack HLL, you will have cracked the Indian market. All the brands in India mimic what HLL does. HLL is the god of Indian advertising.'

So, I put all my energies into cracking Hindustan Lever and began to focus on the brands they sold.

After forty days of trying very hard and making countless phone calls, I managed to get a meeting with the senior brand team in charge of Annapurna Salt. With great trepidation, I met them with my borrowed laptop.

I was greeted by Mr Anil Dua and Mr Gunender Kapur—two fine gentlemen, who patiently heard my pitch. After forty minutes of me continuously gesticulating and speaking excitedly, Mr Kapur said, 'Alok, I love your energy, passion and your idea. It's amazing and innovative. All I need to ask you is one question'.

I was prepared for this. I knew this was 'the' make-or-break question that would make either make me a massively successful entrepreneur or crush me even before I had actually started. I felt like I was in a Mr. Universe competition and was about to be asked the final question that would determine if I would win or lose the crown. With a knotted stomach, I said, 'Sure Sir, ask me ...'

Mr Kapur gently said, 'I like your solution of contests2win, but what's the internet got to do with this?'

I was shocked when I heard that question. That exact moment I understood why I was facing so much resistance getting meetings and doing deals.

I was selling a business idea that was so futuristic, no one could easily imagine it. All I had to do was to make the idea relatable in the present. In my excitement about the internet, that bit had completely skipped me.

When I explained to Mr Kapur that contests2win.com was a website and would encourage consumers to participate in contests, he smiled and said, 'Got it. This is great. Let's do this. We are on.'

That day, I bagged one of the sweetest deals of my life. It was the 9th of July, 1998—a Thursday. As I stepped out of the office of the Hindustan Lever office at Backbay Reclamation at Churchgate, the world outside seemed very different! The birds were singing to me. The evening sun seemed to embrace me with magical warmth. For many months, I had stepped out of infinite pitch meetings feeling complete despair and utter disappointment. That magical day, I felt so alive—as if I had been reborn! And surely enough, it was the day that would change my life forever ...

MY LEARNINGS

I learned that to get a new business off the ground, it takes hard, gruelling, undying, maniacal effort. Every deal in the initial years felt as if I was physically pushing a large airplane from the rear and building speed for it to take off. In my case, I realised that as an entrepreneur trying to solve a new, unfamiliar problem, it was imperative to do lots of research on the industry I was trying to enter. Ideally, I should have familiarised myself with how the industry worked instead of running around like a headless chicken, just making random calls. When I had terrible days as I often did, I felt deficient and regretted not having a better education such as an MBA.

On the positive side, I learned that no matter how uninitiated an entrepreneur is in a new business, one can win customers by focusing on innovation and actual problem-solving. The best lesson I learned from my HLL experience was that even while swimming in an ocean of sceptics and nonbelievers, I persisted in trying to find someone who would believe in me and throw me a lifeline! I hope you will believe me when I tell you that someone out there is waiting for every entrepreneur who dares to try something new and unique. All you have to do is work with all your might and courage, and you will find your true believer.

Free But Not Free

Even while the idea of contests2win.com was very innovative, I believe that its crown jewel was its business model.

When I began pitching to clients for business, I asked myself—what I would pay contests2win.com to host my contests? As a hard-nosed businessman, my intuitive answer was 'nothing', because the concept was untried, untested and unproven. I then wondered that when I, the innovator of the idea was unwilling to pay for my own business proposition, why would others pay for it at all?

This troublesome question made me think up a unique business model for contests2win.com which worked like magic. To all the initial clients I met, I offered my entire range of services—online contest creation, hosting, response management and analytics and winner selection, free of cost. There just was a simple favour that I asked in return. Brands that signed me up needed to promote my contests2win.com link on all their advertising creatives on print, radio, television, hoardings and other media. I pitched this as a simple barter that would not just save the brands money, but also serve as a novel idea to excite and motivate their consumers to participate in their contests in a new, engaging way.

The idea seemed like a no-brainer! Every brand that I signed up readily agreed to this barter. MTV was so excited by this new interactive medium that they got their Video Jockeys to promote my website on the air! My business model was free, but not free.

As I gained momentum with my idea and unique business model, I stumbled across many surprises. The Hollywood Studios in India such as Paramount Pictures, 20th Century Fox, Warner Brothers had insufficient advertising budgets for the many Hollywood movie titles they released through the year. I happily swapped contests with them to provide excellent visibility for their movies, in exchange for plenty of free movie tickets. Jacinto Fernandes of Paramount Pictures became an engaged client, and we would even offer him consumer movie feedback and sentiment analysis of the excitement a movie was generating. As we worked closely and more deeply with movie studios, contests2win. com would poll users on different versions of movie poster creatives for an unreleased movie. The poster most liked by our consumers would be the one printed by the movie company to release in India. A broader value proposition for contests2win was quickly developing.

In the early months of my website launch, I mainly chose to partner brands that were hip, super-urban and premium so as to match the user profile of the first set of internet consumers in India. A sweet lesson I learned was that hosting contests of these top-class brands had a very positive rub-off effect on my brand. By being in the company of great brands, I was being perceived as a great brand myself!

Quickly, consumers began to flock to contests2win. com to win free movie tickets, music CDs, cool t-shirts, interesting memorabilia (a piece of the Berlin Wall, for instance) and super-aspirational prizes (a Mercedes for a day; a cinema theatre reserved for a couple) with just a few clicks of the mouse. By refreshing my contests several times a day, I began to lure consumers to the site daily, and later, even hourly! My website had become a habit for internet consumers in India.

Contest2win.com cooked up the perfect storm. Just a year after starting up, over a hundred of the top brands in India had partnered with us for our innovative, engaging and immersive internet idea. As barter, these brands advertised contests2win on media spend that was worth more than twenty crores (an enormous sum back then). Top brands would sponsor heaps of small, medium and large prizes and we gave away more than one crore rupees worth of prizes to consumers, by the end of our first year. The website began to generate massive buzz, got lots of press and media coverage and became an Indian internet sensation!

MY LEARNINGS

The biggest lesson I learned was to be prudent, practical and street-smart while pitching a business proposition. Many entrepreneurs I knew could not accept giving away their products and service for free. I fought that mindset and did the opposite. The advantage of starting out as a free service meant that I did not have any critical deliverables to be held accountable for. Who would demand anything from something that came complimentary?

For many months, contests2win was a free service that partnered with the world's greatest brands, without having to live up to their stringent expectations or asked to deliver an ROI (Return on Investment) because really, there was no 'I'— Investment! This amazing relationship allowed me to perfect my business, create a deep value proposition for clients and build a great brand for myself. I mastered the art of 'piggyback value creation'. Another deep lesson was understanding the psychological drivers of a business (which exist in every business) and leveraging them to the fullest. In my case, it was the lure of 'free'. Free prizes made consumers go crazy, and they visited my site very frequently looking for free prizes. Soon online contest on contests2win.com had become a habit. And a habit, as I would figure out, was the foundation of a super-successful business model.

The Dog That Got Its Bone

A year after I had started contests2win.com and enjoyed an amazing streak of uninterrupted success, I began to worry about a larger problem that I couldn't ignore, but couldn't do much about. Even though India was a vast market with hundreds of active brands with robust advertising budgets, there weren't enough contests to promote the rapidly growing and ravenous audience I had cultivated on contests2win.com. Thousands of contest seekers would browse the site daily looking for a new contest. When they didn't find any, they would send me nasty feedback. It was a difficult situation and I became desperate to get more contests!

The Hindustan Lever office at Churchgate in South Mumbai became my hunting ground, and I would sit there all day trying to meet (or bump into) the brand managers there hoping to get a contest out of them. One day, I came home looking very haggard and tired. My wife, Chhavi, asked me what was wrong. I said, 'I am the dog in the Hindustan Lever office to whom no one throws a bone ...' Chhavi looked scornfully at me and did not appreciate my comment. At the back of my mind, my intuition told me that there was a larger treasure waiting for me in the corridors of Hindustan Lever. After all, that company spent the largest amounts of money on advertising and promotions every year in India, and it was the ideal hunting ground for me.

One day, maybe out of sheer frustration, when I over-pestered the brand manager of Liril (a popular soap in India) for a contest, he shot back at me angrily. He said, 'Alok, we make soap and shampoos here, not contests. If you want to sell us contests, make some yourself and bring them here.'

That moment, the dark clouds lifted and the thick veil that had been covering my vision was taken away. I knew what I had to do. I had to create contests—not just copy-paste them on my website.

The next day onwards, I began looking for ideas for innovative contests in newspapers, magazines and television media. I was also on the lookout for interesting contests that others were running. My idea was to reach out to the contest creators and try and partner with them. Almost instantly, I spotted some hilarious, irreverent contests hosted on the MTV India Channel. Since I worked with MTV for their client contests, I was swiftly introduced to Cyrus Oshidar—the Creative Director at MTV. In my meeting, I explained to Cyrus the power of interactive digital contests and the amplified engagement they delivered vis-a-vis postcard competitions. I even promised him a token equity share in the business. He caught on to the idea very fast and promised to help me create something interesting.

A couple of days later, Cyrus called me and said, 'Keju, (his first pet name for me; the second is unprintable), let's make a game around a contest. Let's make these consumers play with a brand.'

I listened intently and replied, 'Wow Cyrus ... seems like a good idea. I've just got a brief from Jockey—the innerwear company and the poster they've sent me is a picture of smartly dressed young men and women standing with a tagline "Jockey Inside".'

I cannot ever forget what Cyrus said next. He laughed

and told me, 'Then take their pants down! Create a game in which you put a number below each of these pretty people and make the player choose one correct number that will take down all their pants to reveal their Jockeys. This could be the "Jockey Pants Down Contest". Players will keep trying to get everyone's pants down, and the engagement with the brand and their products will be incredible.'

I gasped at the genius, and sheer innovation of the idea and immediately figured how engaging, and viral this would become. Sure enough Jockey loved the ideas and the 'Jockey Pants down Contest' rocked the internet world when it was launched.

Contests2win.com, Cyrus and I had together created 'advergaming'—a magical blend of advertising and gaming for the entertainment of consumers. I had found my bone, and what a juicy one it was!

MY LEARNINGS

I have learned that if you spend quality time with your clients and consumers, they will point you to what they are looking for. All you have to do is remain super-alert and aware. Often their rebukes and excuses not to do business with you will tell you what you need to do! Another valuable lesson I learned was the value of patience and to be an unapologetic seeker of business. I say this without a hint of embarrassment. If you want to create something unique and valuable, you will have to learn to please and seek. It's a cruel trade-off between your ego and your ambition. You must have the ability to wait endlessly outside people's doors waiting for them to call you inside. It feels humiliating but it is the price you have to pay for enjoying eternal glory.

In the first seven years of starting contests2win. com, this training in waiting bore rich fruit. I became an expert at waiting outside clients' offices for hours just to meet them for as little as five minutes. Never once did I feel bad or humiliated. I became best friends with these busy people's assistants and secretaries and learned a lot about the way their business functioned. 'All good things in life take time' is the tenet I live by. One has to first learn to wait and watch. The win will come in time.

A Knight in Green Armour

While my online contests website contests2win.com had become an instant hit with consumers and top brands in India, I still had a significant hurdle to cross. I needed to generate revenue. Intuitively, I knew that once consumers became hooked to my website, brands would pay me for their contests and promotions as a media channel, just like they did when they hosted their advertisements on other media. While the theory seemed strong, it still had to be put to test.

One afternoon, I received a call from an unknown Bangalore number. The gentleman on the phone was an Ajay Mathur who worked at Intel. He had heard of my website, was visiting Mumbai the next day, and wanted to meet me. Since he was staying at the Oberoi Hotel at Nariman Point, we agreed to meet for breakfast at the Samarkand Coffee Shop. Samarkand was my Dad's favourite coffee shop, and while I loved the restaurant as a startup entrepreneur, I couldn't afford the place. But since someone from Intel had requested for this meeting, I instantly agreed. I had no idea why Ajay had called for the meeting and what his agenda was. By now, I had trained myself to go wherever a client asked me to go.

Ajay turned out to be a nice guy, and we exchanged pleasantries. He told me how deeply impressed he was by the innovative idea of contests2win.com and that Intel endorsed terrific ideas and concepts on the internet—a medium they were actively building their new products for. When the waiter came to take our orders, I ordered a papaya and black coffee (just in case I had to pay the bill). Ajay insisted I join him for the buffet, but I politely declined. Once he returned to the table, Ajay dropped the sweetest bombshell on me. He said, 'Alok, as a token of our appreciation of your entrepreneurial effort and the inventiveness of contests2win.com, Intel would like to purchase a banner position on your website for as long as you would like. We strongly believe in internet startups, and we want to be the first advertiser on contests2win. com. Just quote me a number, and I will get my office to issue you a purchase order the next day.'

I choked on my coffee and began to cry. The act of kindness was overwhelming. Intel had appeared as my knight in green armour to address my biggest business challenge of monetisation almost magically. Instantly I knew that once Intel signed up to be a paying client, others would sign up too, without hesitation. Intel had solved my critical 'proof of concept' dilemma—of generating credible revenue. Ajay handed me his visiting card (one of my most cherished possessions) and said, 'Don't hesitate to do this, Alok. You've earned this business. It's not a favour.'

Back in the office, when I shared this fantastic news with my colleagues. Salil Mahadik—amongst my first and most loyal set of employees said, 'Alok, we have the top banner on the site unused. Let's give that to Intel. They will be the first brand to appear on the site when consumers load the page'.

We quoted a princely sum of rupees five thousand a month to Intel as the cost of hosting the banner on the site, and it was accepted within a few hours. We ran the Intel banner on our website for at least a year before we switched to other advertisers.

MY LEARNINGS

I learned that when an entrepreneur starts to do good work, there are many people including some silent ones who notice. These are the people who will reach out to you proactively to guide, mentor and support you. Just keeping doing good work and the angels will come. I was also blessed to experience that miracles do happen in businesses when you least expect them.

We Want to Buy You Out!

When I was scaling up fast and enjoying a great run with contests2win.com, the most successful internet startup in India at that time was www.rediff.com founded by Ajit Balakrishnan.

Ajit was a living legend for early Indian digital entrepreneurs like myself, and we all watched in awe as he built and scaled revenues, and created absolute top of mind recall for rediff.com in India. He was also the first Indian internet company to issue an IPO on the Nasdaq.

One afternoon, while I was in the office, I received a call from a finance broker from the Dalal Street area in Mumbai. The man spoke in Hinglish and after a few minutes of self-introductions came straight to the point and asked me if I would consider selling contests2win.com to rediff.com.

When I heard his words, the scene from my ultimate fantasy began playing out in my head! In that dream, I had launched a website which had become very famous and successful; soon a wealthy buyer would come along, buy my site and make me very rich. (Notice the lack of mention of revenues, profits or value creation in this dream. This was the quality of the dreams that most internet entrepreneurs had at that time and which some unfortunate ones continue to dream of, even today).

I readily agreed to meet people from rediff.com. In the days before the meeting, I began to build lofty castles in the air of how rich I would become, what I would do with the money and how I would retire (I was thirty years old then).

A meeting was set up at the rediff.com office at Kemps Corner—a stone's throw from my home. When I entered the cold conference room that day, the first person I met was Abhay Havaldar—the highly-regarded venture capitalist who had funded rediff.com and also taken the company public through its IPO on Nasdaq. Abhay is one of the most intelligent, insightful and knowledgeable people I have ever met, and I am eternally grateful for the rediff.com meeting since it gave me the opportunity to get to know him.

A couple of minutes later, as I was settling down, Ajit Balakrishnan entered the room, greeted me and congratulated me on my success with contests2win. As he sat down, Ajit's demeanour changed. He looked very intensely at me and asked, 'Alok, what is the business model of contests2win?'

I did not understand the question because I had not heard the term 'business model' before. Abhay was very perceptive and grinned at me (he has a great grin) when he noticed how perplexed I was by the question. He tried to simplify the question Ajit had asked and said, 'Alok, just tell us how you run this new business you have started.'

I began to ramble about how I would look for clients, create contests for them, procure some of the best prizes in the world and try and make everyone happy. I know my eyes were sparkling when I was saying all of this. Abhay looked at me and continued grinning, while Ajit had switched off. When I finally ended my long monologue, Ajit looked at Abhay and said, 'Alok is running a passion business. This is not for us.'

I was completely crestfallen. I thought I had killed the deal by not being objective in my reply and this was a classic blunder of mine, something I would remember forever. Abhay nodded at Ajit, then softened up as he looked at me and said, 'Alok, you have something great going for you. The passion in you to create contests2win. com is undeniable and infectious! We don't want to ruin your momentum by making you a part of rediff, just yet. You have lots to do, and prove and we think you deserve to do it on your own terms.'

Then Abhay said something that I have never forgotten. He said, 'Alok, you've just begun to run this race a few months back. I want to see your entrepreneurial stamina. Let's see how long you run this race and the distance you go.' What sounded a bit provocative was the most inspiring advice I had ever heard.

I left the rediff office disappointed and broken. When I look back now at that event, I can't help being grateful for the luck that shone on me—of not getting acquired by rediff.com.

MY LEARNINGS

There comes an inflection moment in a startup entrepreneur's life when he receives a reliable signal that he has begun creating value in this business. These signals can come in the form of proactive clients, strategic partnership deals or as inquiries for an acquisition. All of these are important because they validate that the entrepreneur is creating something relevant, interesting and valuable. At times, these are also signs that encourage an entrepreneur to go on and keep pounding the pavements, even when the world at large seems very harsh and dark.

Knock Knock. Who's There? A VC!

On Friday, the busiest day of the week, I received a call on the office landline. I picked up the telephone, and a voice asked: 'Is this Alok?'

I confirmed that it was. The young, excited voice at the other side said, 'This is Gaurav Deepak from ICICI. I've been following your venture contests2win.com and am quite intrigued by it. Do you run it? Is this a business or a hobby? What's the long-term plan? Do you make any revenue? What's the ...' I interrupted Gaurav as he continued to ask critically astute questions and said, 'Boss ... hold on! Who are you and what are all these questions about?'

Gaurav then replied, 'I am part of ICICI Bank's Venture Capital Business. We are funding startups, and this call is to understand what you are doing in your business.' I gulped and tried to give him some replies on the phone. We then agreed to meet a couple of days later at the ICICI Building at Bandra Kurla Complex (BKC), Mumbai.

If you've been to the ICICI building at BKC, you will agree that its grandeur and sheer presence is uplifting and inspiring. I felt pleased as I strode into the building to meet Gaurav. The building seemed to be welcoming me as a long-term partner.

In a cozy wood-panelled room, I met Gaurav and his boss Pratibha Ashok. They were very courteous and enquired about the business and my plans for it. This was my first ever VC meeting, and I was ill-prepared for it. Neither was I a 'VC-smart' entrepreneur (knowing what to say to VCs) nor was I trained to be articulate in describing my business, its key metrics, and drivers. Just as Ajit Balakrishnan had figured out when I had met them in a discussion for rediff.com to buy out contests2win.com, Gaurav and Pratibha at ICICI too understood that I was running contests2win with unstoppable passion and commitment, but was not strategically thinking of my business and planning for its long-term growth, scale, and sustainability.

Gaurav asked me, 'Alok, do you have a business plan? We would love to look at one.' I gulped and said, 'Sure, let me send you something tomorrow.'

Gaurav raised his eyebrows when I said 'send you something tomorrow' but did not probe further. I left the ICICI building excited and helpless. A couple of days later, I sent Gaurav my 'business plan'. It was a two-page word document that described why contests2win.com was so great. There was nothing else in it.

Gaurav asked for another meeting, and we met at the ICICI building once again. Gaurav politely said, 'Alok, this is not a business plan. This is worse than toilet paper. Please don't show this to anyone.' I was shattered when I heard this. I had no clue what to do or ask. Just then Gaurav said, 'Alok, would you like us to recommend someone to you who could help you write a business plan to help you with investors?' I immediately agreed, and the next day Gaurav introduced me to Sushanto Mitra—the second messiah in my life.

Sushanto was a banker who smoked like a chimney, ate Lay's chips and drank black coffee for dinner and transformed his jaw into a perfect square whenever he had a bright idea. We sat together for forty nights in my

Nana's old transport office that was now the contests2win office, with vampire-like mosquitoes and scurrying rats for company and thrashed out a detailed business plan for contests2win.

A few days later, I submitted this to ICICI and waited for their response. One late afternoon, Sushanto called me and said, 'Alok, there is a new VC in town. They call themselves eVentures. They seem like solid guys. Would you like to meet them?' I instantly agreed.

I met Rajesh Jog and Neeraj Bhargava of eVentures in the small coffee shop of a new bookshop that had just opened in town near Mahalaxmi Temple called Crossword. Meeting in cute coffee shops was my standard operating procedure. When a meeting was being planned, I would pretend to have a prior meeting in a posh hotel near the client and request them to meet me at that hotel. I did this so that clients and partners would never have to visit my old, rat-infested office. The New Oberoi lobby's sunken coffee area in Mumbai operated as my office for many years. The Taj Mumbai hotel management, on the contrary, was quite nasty and always shooed me away.

The two gentlemen from eVentures were in suits; I was in a tee and jeans. Rajesh Jog reached out and shook my hand. If you've met Rajesh Jog once, you can't forget him. He makes his presence felt. The big shuffle, the sharp banker appearance, the George Clooney smile and the Dara Singh handshake, all leave their mark. Neeraj Bhargava, on the other hand, was very subtle and subdued in his interaction. He kept watching me intently and asked some brilliant questions. I was very impressed by Neeraj. After discussing the basics of my business, Rajesh and Neeraj asked me,

'Alok, why should we invest in you?' I took my time to reply. My mind whizzed past all the curated 'VC perfect' replies that I had read which I could have chosen. I again felt like Mr Universe being asked the golden question on stage to make or break his chance.

A minute later, I said something I never imagined I would. I looked at Neeraj, smiled and said, 'Why should you invest in me? Well, that's for you to figure out. You guys are VCs and who knows better than you?' That was a very 'anti-VC' reply to give out, but I intuitively felt I needed to show some attitude. My hunch was to be proven right.

A week later, Sushanto called me excitedly. He said, 'Alok, both ICICI and eVentures want to invest in contests2win. com. What do you want to do?'

I was confused. I liked Neeraj a lot, but ICICI was a great brand and Gaurav Deepak at ICICI was amazing too. Of all the people that came to my mind, I called Ajit Balakrishnan—the founder of rediff.com for advice. I knew he would be my best sounding board. Ajit said, 'Alok, ICICI has the money but lack the insights. eVentures has the insights but doesn't have money.' When I asked him to clarify, Ajit explained saying e-Ventures were still raising their venture fund and their money wouldn't be in their bank for at least six more months.

I decided to split my raise between the two companies and just as Ajit had predicted, I received the ICICI money immediately after signing, but the eVentures cash came precisely six months later.

MY LEARNINGS

Trust me when I say that when an entrepreneur starts doing something innovative, disruptive and compelling, capital begins to chase the entrepreneur, as opposed to the entrepreneur having to chase capital earlier. There are billions of dollars sitting idle with investors all over the world, all waiting for the ideal entrepreneur with a solid business idea.

During my VC rounds, I realised how crucial it was for the entrepreneur to narrate an immersive story, present a detailed, meaningful business plan and to be able to sell himself as much as his business while attempting to raise money. As the years have unfolded, I have learned how important it is for an entrepreneur to choose his investors wisely. That decision should be treated with the same care and sensitivity as when selecting a spouse. VC stands for Venture Capital, but it could well mean Vapour Capital, Vulture Capital and Vampire Capital. It is important for the entrepreneur to choose a VC with the utmost prudence.

Beauty Lies in the
Eyes of the Financier

After I had signed on the term sheets to obtain funding by eVentures and ICICI, exhaustive due diligence began on my business and its operations. Beyond studying my company documents and auditing my accounts (there was hardly anything to examine), the diligence was on my leadership capabilities and my vision to build the business.

At the eVentures office at Khetan Bhavan at Churchgate, I met Neeraj Bhargava again, this time in a stately boardroom. Neeraj was very focused and unnerved me with his penetrating stare. I was nervous, to say the least.

Without pleasantries, Neeraj said, 'Alok, we have been thinking of the contests2win business and have two major issues to discuss. If we cannot resolve these, we may not be able to fund you.' My heart began to beat very fast. This was a meeting I did not want to mess up.

Neeraj said, 'My first question is about revenue. You have not charged your clients for any of the work you have done for them, despite partnering with some of the biggest and most reputed marketers in India. The second issue is about your team and the lack of anyone credible in there, other than yourself. How do you propose to tackle these issues?'

Having experienced several meetings that did not go well, I had learned a hard lesson that mumbling stupid answers was worse than keeping quiet. I remained silent for a few seconds, gathered my thoughts and said, 'Neeraj, I am building an amazing new business that has never existed in the world before. It's helping brands and consumers in an unprecedented way. A value will be derived from it.'

Neeraj nodded and sternly asked me, 'How many people do you have in contests2win? What are their qualifications?'

I meekly replied, 'I have two web designers and a marketing and sales guy from a not so well-known B-School in the team.'

Neeraj scowled a bit and then said something that took me by complete surprise. He said, 'Let me put your brand connections to the test. Write down your top ten brand contacts with their phone numbers on a sheet of paper, and let me call them right now and ask them about you and your team. Make sure to list the brand owners who have given you repeat business; not just single-deal clients who may have been swayed by your sweet talk.'

I was cornered and meekly did what I was asked to do. I wrote down the names of the clients who were doing the most amount of contests with contests2win. These included Paramount Pictures, Hindustan Lever, MTV, etc. After a moment's hesitation, I also wrote down the name of Thota Ranganath (Ranga) of Pepsi who had given me lots of business but was my most challenging client. His demands would make my team and me literally tear our hair out. I was not sure if he would say good things about me, but he was undoubtedly a massive volume client.

Neeraj glanced at the list very carefully and as luck would have it, chose to call Ranga. As he began dialling, my heart sank yet again. I heard Neeraj asking Ranga questions like, 'Do you deal with contests2win? How is their work? Do you like the team?' He then asked, 'Why don't you compensate them?'

Ranga's reply made Neeraj get up and walk out of the room. It was almost ten minutes later that Neeraj came back into the room. Those few minutes of waiting seemed like a year to me. But when he came back, he had a smile on his face!

Neeraj then grinned at me and said, 'Alok, Ranga told me that he loves your ideas and your work.' He then paused and continued, 'I asked Ranga the reason why Pepsi didn't compensate contests2win.com for all the good work that it provided. Ranga told me 'Alok never asks and added that Pepsi was worried if there was something fraudulent about contests2win because no agency or partner worked with Pepsi complimentary!'

In the end, Neeraj said something that completely shook me up. He said, 'I also asked Ranga if he would ever consider working for contests2win and with Alok. Ranga replied, "Of course! It sounds fascinating!"'

That moment, I realised the absolute truth in the statement that top-notch VCs provide tons of strategic guidance, hiring insights, connections, and business assistance that far outweighs the money they invest in an entrepreneur's startup.

After the funding process was complete, Ranga actually joined contests2win.com as my Chief Operating Officer (COO) and later went on to launch Mobile2win in China as the founder of that business.

MY LEARNINGS

I learned that it was imperative for entrepreneurs to engage with experienced mentors and investors, and have them ask tough, hard-hitting, even upsetting questions about the entrepreneur's businesses and value she is creating. I realised that an entrepreneur must be bold, forthright and demanding of revenues when building a business. I was hesitant to ask clients for money because I was afraid of losing them. Neeraj demystified my fear in a single conversation—something that I could have done much earlier, but held back because I was fearful. Finally, I learned that an entrepreneur meets many accomplished people while conducting his business, and some of them can be motivated to become a part of the entrepreneur's team by just asking! An entrepreneur must develop the confidence and courage to seek partners confidently and without hesitation when he thinks they are the right people to partner with. Being meek and reserved are qualities unbecoming of an entrepreneur.

A Personal Blunder

After the due diligence for funding contests2win.com was complete, I spent considerable time reviewing and then finally, accepted the sharehclding and share subscription agreements ICICI and eVentures sent me. It was decided that I would first execute the complete set of documents with eVentures, to be immediately followed by ICICI. Neeraj Bhargava of eVentures suggested that we meet in the lobby of the New Oberoi hotel on the evening of the 26th of October to sign them. I gulped when I heard the date because it was my wife Chhavi's birthday and I was keen on spending the evening with her. Chhavi was also pregnant at that time and it was all the more important that I spend that evening with her.

Over the previous eighteen months, when I had been building contests2win.com, I had spent a lot of time away from Chhavi and my family and was planning to make it up to her on her birthday. But when Neeraj suggested the 26th, I immediately accepted. Somewhere, a voice in my head said, 'Chhavi's birthday comes every year; funding comes once in a lifetime, so don't be stupid and just say "Yes".'

As destiny would have it, my younger daughter was born on Sunday, the 24th of October. I chuckled and told Chhavi, 'My daughter is so kind, she knows her Dad is a busy entrepreneur and so decided to be born on a holiday.' At the hospital, everything went well and the doctors decided to discharge Chhavi and my daughter on the 26th of October at 5 p.m. That was the same time and date that had been agreed upon between Neeraj and me at eVentures to sign the final funding documents of contests2win.com.

I decided to skip going to the hospital and requested my parents to go instead, while I sat in the Oberoi lobby signing my funding documents. When Neeraj courteously asked me about my family, I told him about the birth of my younger daughter. He congratulated me and was quite surprised to note that I was sitting with him instead of being with my family. We completed the signing of the documents by 7 p.m., and I headed home.

Late in the evening, as I sat at home, I felt very disappointed and disheartened on a day that I should have been at my happiest. I had signed the funding documents, and my newly-born daughter had just arrived home! But, Neeraj's surprised look in the hotel lobby kept playing in my mind. I had stupidly sacrificed a golden, once-in-a-lifetime family moment for a business transaction that could have easily been delayed by a day. That night, after I had kissed my newborn baby and Chhavi good night, I swore to myself that everything I would do henceforward would be prioritised keeping my family's happiness first.

Chhavi has never forgiven me for being absent for one of the most precious moments of our life together. It is something that I live with.

MY LEARNINGS

As I mature, I have learned that even though fame, fortune and glory are important, it is utterly futile and silly for an entrepreneur to sacrifice precious personal moments to chase transient business events. I believe that a person's highest success is best demonstrated by the happiness of the people closest to him. The most significant lesson for me was that everything else could wait when it comes to one's family and their happiness.

Children Have to Fall to Learn to Walk

Business at contests2win.com had scaled up very well. Ranga from Pepsi had joined us as Chief Operating Officer, and he was on fire! He was leading business development and sales and was creating massive traction for the company. Cyrus Oshidar of MTV regularly came into the office and helped me build the entire art and creative team from scratch in his role as a mentor. We were killing it with ideas and 'wow' 'adver-games' that clients loved. I had even convinced Gopala Krishna (GK) to also join me as Chief Technology Officer (CTO). Someone in the team commented, 'Alok has got the Holy Trinity of Brahma, Vishnu, and Mahesh to work for him.'

Then 2001 happened. That was the year when the 'internet bubble' burst. The year when 'dot-com' became 'dot gone'. The internet suddenly seemed to be a bad word, and everyone associated with it began to get treated like pariahs.

Contests2win.com was in a good place. We had begun aggressively charging for our services and had discontinued our barter model. Ranga had created a 'Rate Card' for the company and made it a rule for the sales team to collect fifty per cent advance for all the deals we closed. Clients were used to paying advances to their advertising agencies for their creative production work and readily agreed to pay us. We were generating real revenues in the year 2001—an unheard-of scenario for internet startups back then (for some, even now). But the total cash we were spending on salaries, travel, and technology still exceeded the revenues we were generating.

The company needed more money, and I turned to ICICI for help. My other VC, eVentures had also been affected by the dot-com crash and had ceased operations a few months later, that year. Renuka Ramnath and Bala Deshpande were now in charge of ICICI Ventures, and I managed to get a meeting with them for GK and myself. The venue was once again at the Oberoi. I still remember the sofa we sat on—the one next to the piano in the lobby area. That sofa was meant to accommodate a single person, but GK and I squeezed into it, literally sitting on the 'edge'.

When Renuka and Bala arrived, I began the conversation and rambled a bit about how contests2win.com was growing and how our business was scaling. Then I looked at Renuka and said, 'Ma'am, we need more money to grow. Can you please help us with a small round of funding just to tide us over for the next year or so?'

Renuka kept silent for a long while and then looked at me, smiled and said, 'Alok, when we have small children, they fall when they start walking. As parents, we can easily prevent them from falling, but we don't. Allowing them to fall is what teaches them to walk.' That's all that Renuka said! She then signalled to Bala, and both of them left the meeting.

GK and I were shell-shocked. Our only hope of raising funds had vanished on the back of a Zen-style philosophy statement that had lasted for less than ten seconds. We both left the hotel feeling wretched. I had knots in my stomach and felt like throwing up.

Things didn't look good.

MY LEARNINGS

I bitterly learned that the best-laid plans could go up in smoke when the wind changes direction. Nothing was certain in business and a hero today could quickly become a zero tomorrow. We were lucky that we had started generating revenues as compared to the other more popular portals of that time that had not yet figured out how to make money. Those websites vanished in a few weeks after the dot-com bust because they had been late in getting down to generating cash flow. In a down market, no one wanted to risk spending their money on them. The VC debacle taught me about the fickle nature of money and how one could never assume that it would always be available. I decided never to build a business by relying solely on venture capital funding. This incident also helped me evolve a vital caveat of mine: 'You never get money when you most want it, but it's always available when you least need it.'

We Are Looking in the Wrong Place

I was shattered when ICICI refused to extend a fresh round of capital for contests2win.com, despite us doing so well and proving to them that we were a revenue-generating internet business, on the path to profitability.

At that moment, it seemed like the world was collapsing around us. None of the VCs who were so eager to fund us a few months back wanted to touch anything that had the word dot-com in it. As an entrepreneur, I had built a great business, had over 150 of the Fortune 500 brands as clients and partners, had assembled one of the best teams in the world and built a platform that was revolutionary and disruptive; yet, there was no one to give us money just to help us survive!

To preserve cash, GK, Ranga and I halved our salaries. GK and I went further and even stopped collecting those reduced salaries from the company. The sales funnel began worsening because the hot dot-com clients that gave us juicy, lucrative deals were fast disappearing. I was extremely anxious; I travelled to Mahabaleshwar (a hill station near Mumbai) with Chhavi and our kids just to escape the trauma of going to work every day. My anxiety became worse there. I called Dinesh Gopalakrishnan (my most loyal and trusted colleague who is still with me) and rambled about how we would have to close the company down and quit the business. He merely told me to take it easy, relax and come back refreshed to the office.

After I returned from my Mahabaleshwar trip, on a

depressing Monday, I calculated that we had just four months of cash left in the company to pay salaries and expenses. I asked GK to meet me in the small conference room of the office to decide on our next steps. The room was dark and warm. We would shut off the air-conditioning and lights during lunch hours to save money. I explained the dire situation to GK, and we agreed on a broad strategy. We decided to lay off most of our employees while maintaining a bare existence and a skeletal team.

GK said, 'Alokji, after this month's salary, let's send a mail to everyone telling them to resign and to start looking for new jobs. We will promise them salaries for the next two months.' I desperately said, 'GK, isn't there something else we can do? I mean we still have four months of cash left.'

GK eyes twinkled as he slowly looked around the dark conference room. I saw his gaze land on a large-sized contests2win logo cut out that was placed on the window of the conference room. The contests2win.com logo was a giant hand decorated with all the logos of the brands we had worked with.

GK suddenly began smiling while still looking at the contests2win logo and slowly turned towards me. With his shining eyes he said, 'Alokji, we have been meeting the wrong people for funding! We have been pitching to the wrong people. We have been looking in the wrong direction, all this while! We have to think that our corporate clients are our VCs, no one else! You need to double and triple your efforts and get more business from real-world clients. Please stop wasting your time in chasing fence-sitting VCs who will do nothing for us. You need to get the business funded by business cash flow, not through investments.

Investments will not happen now, but business will always happen!'

In my entire career upto that point, those words were the most divine words I had ever heard. The moment GK made his point, it felt as if an electric current had passed through my body. A warm glow enveloped me. I felt that once again my Lord Krishna has spoken from the lips of Gopala Krishna. I looked at GK and said nothing. I just smiled.

That day onwards, sales became my karma and my dharma. It was the only thing I did and focused on. I made it mandatory for all the salespeople in the team including myself to meet three clients every day, come what may. We went on a complete sales frenzy, without sounding too desperate or anxious when engaging with our clients. GK broke the numbers down very neatly for all of us. He explained that we needed ten deals a month to survive on our own. Since the conversion in our business was about ten per cent, that meant that we had to meet a hundred clients a month to make sure we met our sales targets.

Over the course of the next five years, I reached out to over three thousand clients personally and got lucrative business from many of them. We never incurred a loss from that month onwards, and our business became self-sustaining and profitable.

MY LEARNINGS

The hardest times provide the most excellent moments of clarity. As an entrepreneur, anything and everything is possible if you put your heart and soul into it. The most important lesson was about the critical and vital role of sales in a business. Without the ability to sell what you create, everything goes downhill, beyond a point. A key learning was that a founder must roll up his sleeves and jump straight into the heart of the business problem. Sitting on the sidelines giving instructions to the teams doesn't help. In contests2win.com, sales was key to survival. So, I decided to become the greatest salesperson the startup world had ever seen!

Why Don't You Guys
Come to China?

As stated previously, one of my VCs, eVentures had been
severely affected by the dot-com bust and had shut shop
in India. But even as they were exiting, a parting gift they
left me with was a strong introduction to Softbank, who
happened to be one of their investors. (VCs have investors
too!) Softbank is one of the largest and most successful
investors in internet and mobile businesses in the world.

Softbank was intrigued by and impressed with our
business model. Since our quarterly reports reached them
via eVentures, they were aware that we were a dot-com
company that was generating revenue and had world-class
clients. On a conference call with the global Softbank teams,
one of their directors asked, 'Alok, why don't you guys
come to China? China is just like India. Chinese internet
users also like to win prizes through games, gambling, and
contests. The contests2win business model can easily work
there. And we can incubate you in our office in China.'

Honestly, I had no clue about the state of affairs in China.
All I knew from media reports and local businessmen I met
was that the Chinese were hostile competitors and went
ruthlessly after anyone who competed with them. Wherever
Chinese products went, local products got wiped out. Given
this brutal backdrop, I wondered why I was being asked to
take my company to China?

I mentioned the Softbank offer to Ranga. Ranga's face
brightened up when he heard this and he spontaneously

said, 'Alok, this is a no-brainer. China provides the scale we are looking for. I will go there and start up the business myself. I have only one condition. To discuss the China business plan, instead of us going to Shanghai, I insist that the Softbank folks come to India to meet us. I want to make sure that they want us as badly as we want them; their trip to Mumbai will serve as a confirmation.'

I was shocked at Ranga's willingness to move to China and set up the business there. But knowing his relentless drive and deep commitment, I agreed to take the discussion forward and invited the Softbank team to visit us in Mumbai. A couple of weeks later, Peter Hua and his colleague came over to our office, discussed the business plan and shook hands with us to set up contests2win.com China as a 50-50 Joint Venture between Softbank China and contests2win. com.

The very next day, Ranga asked two of our star employees—Ranjit Singh and Ravi Bose to pack their bags for a quick trip to China. Ranjit's story has become something of a legend in contests2win.com. He asked Ranga, 'How many days do you think I will be gone for?' Ranga replied, 'Pack for a couple of weeks, and then we will see.' As I write this in 2018, Ranjit is still in China. His two weeks have become seventeen years!

Softbank China played a fantastic role as a partner and incubated us in an elegant building on Jiangsu Road in Shanghai. Ranga set up the office there with Ranjit and Ravi. A few months later, Ranga moved his family to Shanghai and settled down in the city for the long haul.

By the time contests2win.com began business deployment in China, the internet craze in that country had peaked. There were several large companies there that had built large consumer-facing businesses and competing with them seemed impossible. I still remember the names of Sohu, Sina, and Netease being mentioned in almost every conversation when the China teams discussed business and consumer activation ideas. While the internet business was overly competitive, the market around mobile content and engagement had just begun to take off. At that time, China had about three hundred million mobile users who had begun using the first set of 'feature phones' (an early version of what later came to be called the 'smartphone') that companies like Nokia had successfully introduced in the market.

Ranga spotted a significant opportunity with these devices and convinced Softbank and me to rechristen 'contests2win China' as 'Mobile2win China' and start a contests business for brands on mobile phones via SMS messaging services instead of going the online route as we had in India. Both Softbank and I readily agreed because Ranga's plan seemed logical and built for the future. Once we gave our green signal, Ranga worked like a demon, and within a short period achieved a few impossible things. He toured the entire country of China and signed up all the local operators to allot a four-digit shortcode (8558) to Mobile2win China as a short code for mobile contesting. Shortcodes, as you may have noticed, are short four-five digit easy to remember numbers that consumers can send specific SMS messages to. As opposed to typing long ten digit telephone numbers that are not easy to recall, they make it easy for consumers to message. Ranga managed to sign up many top Fortune 500 global brands for our

SMS contests delivered through our platform to promote themselves on the 8558 short code service. He also convinced many brands to promote our short code on their television commercials to activate consumer participation, just as I had done with top brands when I had started contests2win.com!

In less than two years, the business of Mobile2win China had scaled up extremely well. We had signed up most of the leading brands operating in China. Their aggressive media campaign that included advertising our 8558 short code on television commercials had generated millions of SMS responses. These SMS messages generated revenues for Mobile2win.com and Chinese mobile operators. Our Mobile2win China business had started in earnest.

But even as Mobile2win China was earning SMS revenues and brand fees, the company was still bleeding cash due to the high cost of the salaries being paid out, the cost of renting servers and implementing technologies to build a robust SMS platform. The initial money that contests2win India and Softbank China had invested in the business would soon be exhausted, and the company had to raise capital fast.

A year after Mobile2win China was launched, we received an investment inquiry from Siemens Mobile—a division of the massive global conglomerate Siemens. Siemens Mobile had a strategic investment arm called 'Siemens Mobile Acceleration' (SMAC) and their business model was to invest in mobile entertainment startups to help roll out innovations and ideas to propel their mobile handsets business. After a few conversations with Ranga and the Mobile2win China team, SMAC offered to invest. When the board sent me the term sheet, I agreed to it without a second thought. The trauma of almost running out of money at contests2win.com still haunted me, and I knew how difficult it would be for an Indian firm to raise capital for its China division. The brand name of Siemens itself was a big motivation. All that passed through my mind was that 'beggars can't be choosers' as I signed the term sheet. As I soon came to realise, it was a strategic mistake.

MY LEARNINGS

I always thought of VCs to be financial investors, but the partnership, funding and active participation by Softbank to set up our China business showed me how truly supportive, hands-on and valuable a VC relationship could be if they had the ability to incubate and launch startup businesses. In the event that startup entrepreneurs have a choice to choose between multiple VCs, they should consider giving extra points to those VCs who could help in executing their business as opposed to those who are only interested in funding the business. The success of Ranga in China and his flawless execution in kickstarting a difficult, new-age business in a hostile country taught me that an entrepreneur must strive to hire people better than himself to be his partners. I learned that nothing was impossible if you have an innovative and disruptive business idea—not even going to a super-competitive market like China and competing with the Chinese!

All's Well That Ends Well!

One of my biggest mistakes as an entrepreneur was inviting a strategic investor Siemen Mobile Accelerator (SMAC) to fund Mobile2win China instead of a financial investor. Simply explained, a strategic investor is someone who invests in a company or startup with a specific business intention. Strategic investors are usually large corporations (like Siemens) who make investments in line with their own corporate business plans. They often play an active role in the management of the company they fund. In our case, Siemens was interested in Mobile2win China to support its own handset mobile phone business that it had recently launched.

Financial investors on the other hand invest to make multiple times returns on their money. They play an active role in helping the funded company find more investors and exit opportunities, but they rarely participate in the management of the business. Financial investors have a simple, single-point agenda—to make the maximum money possible and get out. Strategic investors on the other hand gradually acquire the company they invest in (if things go as per plan) or lose interest in the company if plans don't work out.

After Siemen Mobile Accelerator (SMAC) invested into Mobile2win China, they got involved in the operations of the company and wanted us to adhere to the best practices of their parent organisation. For instance, SMAC wanted the China office to start early in the morning because that is how Siemens operated in Germany. SMAC wanted our staff to follow their German HR protocols, which included extra holidays and perks, six months of maternity and paternity schemes and other benefits that were unaffordable for startups like Mobile2win China. They requested the CEO to report to the SMAC board members and discuss business strategies with them.

So far, before the SMAC investment, we had had operated Mobile2win China without any instructions from Softbank and when SMAC got involved, the teams got rattled. One day, I received a message from Ranga telling me that he had decided to move on. That was one of the saddest days in my life, but deep in my heart I realised that Ranga preferred to work in a startup because it had a free, protocol-less environment instead of a control centric corporate atmosphere. I immediately requested our CTO, Gopala Krishnan (GK) from Mumbai to take over the Chinese operations and he was kind enough to oblige.

I was shocked to learn that within a few weeks, Siemens and Softbank had significant issues with GK. I soon received a cryptic one-line message from Softbank China asking me to be present for the next Mobile2win board meeting in Shanghai. I had never been asked to be present for a Mobile2win China board meeting, and instinctitively, this sounded like trouble.

In Shanghai, the night before the board meeting, I accepted a dinner invitation from the board members from Softbank and SMAC. We met at Va Bene—a famous Italian restaurant in the Xintiandi district of Shanghai. When I suggested we share a bottle of wine (I used to drink back then), the other two gentlemen kept noticeably quiet. Just as I had suspected, clearly, something was amiss. This was by no means going to be a friendly meal.

After the dinner was over and we were getting ready to leave, the SMAC Board member spoke up and said, 'Alok, thanks for coming to Shanghai for the board meeting. Softbank and we have been having discussions about GK and how he is managing the business. It is in a sad state.'

I replied, 'That's not what GK tells me. Even so, I completely respect your views. Let us all discuss the issues in detail in our board meeting tomorrow.'

Then, the Softbank person spoke up and said, 'Well, there is no scope for that. We are firing GK at the board meeting tomorrow. This dinner was just to tell you about our decision since you are the founder-entrepreneur of the company and we owed you this information in advance.' I gulped, and before I could protest, both gentlemen got up from the table, signalling the end of all discussions.

The moment I was in a taxi, I called GK and asked him to meet me near the apartment complex where I was staying. I appraised GK of the meeting, and we debated on the strategy for the board meeting. I intuitively knew that that firing GK was not feasible because there was no one else left to run the company. Either my Board members were testing my sentiments for GK, or they were subtly coercing me to go along with their wishes. After spending a lot of time debating on many 'what if' situations, I told GK to be calm and composed, and even if the investors did propose a firing resolution, the two of us would object to it as board members. I was keen to figure out what was brewing in the minds of Softbank and SMAC.

The Mobile2win board meeting was supposed to start at

10 a.m. and GK and I stuffed ourselves with a super-heavy breakfast. We both knew that this was going to be a hostile meeting and none of the investors would arrange for lunch for us, perhaps as a tactic to wear us down. The board meeting started at ten sharp and ended at four without any breaks in between. Lunch was neither ordered nor served.

The board meeting was something that I will never forget. It was wild and chaotic. On one side, the SMAC investors would speak to each other in German and reply back to us in English. GK and I spoke in Hindi as we prepared our retorts. The Softbank team kept talking in Chinese while discussing their ideas internally. SMAC held GK responsible for not scaling up the business, even though he had taken charge of the Company just a few weeks ago. Softbank mentioned that GK was doing questionable deals to report revenue growth and reprimanded him for it. While replying to a point made by Softbank, GK pointed the finger at one of their representatives. This upset the Softbank Board member very much. He looked very sternly at GK and said, 'Never point a finger at me.' I later learned that pointing fingers was terrible etiquette in China. The nonstop discussion continued for hours, and when the meeting ended, there was no resolution moved to fire GK. It seemed the board meeting was meant to be nothing more than a marathon business discussion for the management team and I was called in to serve as the witness. Both GK and I left the meeting feeling strangely elated! We celebrated our mini-victory that night in a bar overlooking the Bund.

Intuitively, we both knew that unhappy investors would not stay quiet for long and the status quo was not going to last. When SMAC and Softbank again hinted that we needed to change GK, I agreed with them. Both the investors managed to hire a smart lady called Irene Wu as the CEO of Mobile2win. GK was allowed to stay on as Director to help her in the business. I felt relieved that we had gained some more breathing time.

Irene was a smart lady and did an excellent job of making the board feel comfortable. She worked with GK to stabilise the business, but she wasn't the passionate entrepreneur that a startup company like Mobile2win China needed. Irene managed to keep the company's business at a cruising level, without too much of an uplift. A few months later, Irene visited India, and I invited her to meet my family over dinner. The next day in the office, she told me that while she loved the innovative and disruptive business of Mobile2win, she wasn't happy working in a company with a dysfunctional board. She had decided to move on.

Soon, Mobile2win China was back to square one— without a CEO and with an acrimonious board that took nasty swipes at each other. Via email, my investors informed me that they proposed hiring the global firm Heidrick and Struggles to look for a CEO for the company. Heidrick and Struggles is a worldwide heavyweight in the headhunting business, and their costs would be exorbitantly expensive for a small startup such as Mobile2win China. I knew that their fees could dent the company's cash reserves and I refused to sign the board resolution for the headhunting contract. The investors were upset, but this time the ball was in my court, and I refused to play along with them. Frustrated by me, the investors wrote out their own contract with Heidrick and Struggles and got them on board for the CEO staffing job.

Just a month later, GK informed me that a gentleman called Nick Zhang sourced via Heidrick & Struggles had been appointed as the new CEO of Mobile2win China. Nick was from Linktone—a mobile entertainment company that had been recently listed on Nasdaq. Nick's specialisation was turning around mobile startup companies and GK sounded very impressed by him. I once again breathed a sigh of relief.

While Nick began to revitalise Mobile2win China, he leveraged the excellent work done by Ranga—the founder of Mobile2win and the COO of contests2win.com. Ranga had laid the foundation of a very solid SMS messaging platform at Mobile2win China by partnering with all the local Chinese mobile operators with our proprietary mobile shortcode 8558. The top advertisers of China had actively begun using this platform, and The Walt Disney Company was one of our top clients. Mobile2win's innovative mobile business model of creating engaging contests and brand promotions later became a Stanford University case study.

A few months after Nick had joined as CEO, I noticed a mail from Siemens in my inbox. As I clicked on it, I was sure my investors were done with Nick Zhang this time and wanted to fire him. Instead, I saw one of the most beautiful messages I had ever read in my life. The email read, 'Alok, we have good news. The Walt Disney Company has made a generous offer to purchase Mobile2win China for an all-cash deal. We have decided to sell and assume you will agree too. Please revert with your consent so that we can proceed with the transaction.'

I couldn't believe my eyes as I reread and reread the message over and over again. Mobile2win China had been in a near-death situation for almost two years, and all that I had hoped for was for its survival. I had never imagined that a company like Disney would acquire it!

I quickly sent my consent to Siemens, and Mobile2win China was acquired by Disney. The money we received delivered us a six times returns on our original investment, besides giving me the immortal glory of being an entrepreneur who had sold his company to Disney! This was a magical dream that had come true for me.

MY LEARNINGS

The Mobile2win China experience really taught me about how an entrepreneur should carefully choose his investors and align his interests with the agenda of his investors, to succeed. Financial investors are ideal partners in the early stages of a startup and strategic investors are best suited to come in towards the end (as potential acquirers too). I believe that Siemens was justified in trying to operate and control Mobile2win China since they were strategic investors who wanted the business to operate within the do's and don'ts of their corporate framework. I should have been more aware and prepared my team for business process changes after we decided to get funded by Siemens. The appointment of Nick Zhang was a very interesting learning for me. I had always despised expensive consultants and their elaborate proposals, but the success of Heidrick and Struggles in hiring the perfect CEO for the Mobile2win China business taught me that there was a reason why the world's top companies worked with such consultants. They delivered and really created value for their clients. More so, I learned that startup founders were not always right. In this case, I would never have hired Heidrick and Struggles, but the VCs did, and that decision catalysed the sale of Mobile2win China to Walt Disney.

The sale of the business also made me realise that even though operationally, startups can be very troubled and often badly messed up, the value they create through their struggle and strife is often attractive to external acquirers (in our case none other than The Walt Disney Company). Entrepreneurs can rejoice in knowing that all the pain, trauma and suffering they endure will surely pay off if they stick to their plan and keep executing, till the very end!

Mobile2win India

Just as Mobile2win China began to gain business momentum and traction, Ranga and I decided to launch Mobile2win India. We knew that the mobile consumer revolution that had started sweeping China would inevitably replicate itself in India and we thought it was best to begin the Mobile2win business model in India at the earliest. Laterally, Ranga also made me compete with him. We both wanted to build huge businesses in the countries that we operated in.

In an earlier chapter, I had spoken about how I was very good at playing the waiting game—sitting outside client offices for business and meetings. It was at the Shaw Wallace offices at Ballard Estate, Mumbai where I waited for the longest. The marketing directors sometimes made me wait for hours for a single meeting. During this waiting 'tapasya' (penance), I met a gentleman called Rajiv Hiranandani who worked at Yahoo! India. Rajiv was a great salesman, and we would keep bumping into each other in different offices across the country as we competed hard to sell our respective internet services. When the Mobile2win India plans started firming up, I met up with Rajiv, pitched to him the massive opportunity Mobile2win India offered and got him to come onboard as the COO of Mobile2win India.

Soon, Rajiv and I swung into business development mode and began meeting media companies and brands to pitch the idea of mobile contests to them to engage consumers. The Mobile2win model was similar to the contests2win pitch except that this time the service was powered by SMS on mobile instead of a website.

While we were pitching mobile engagement, Star India (a top television channel) launched a brand new, revolutionary television show called 'KBC—Kaun Banega Crorepati' which was the Indian equivalent of a global hit show called 'Who Wants to Be a Millionaire'. KBC quickly became the most popular television programme in India. The show offered a prize of rupees one crore which was an unbelievable sum of money to win in a television contest! It also raced up the rating charts because it featured the iconic Indian actor, Amitabh Bachchan as the show anchor. While KBC was a massive hit, a significant challenge with the show was its inefficient method of enlisting show participants. To qualify, contestants needed to call the Star TV India landline and answer a few questions. The challenge was that the telephone number was forever busy, and contestants would sometimes be redialling the number for hours without success. This was a massive consumer irritant.

I noticed this last mile problem with the KBC show and approached Star India pitching our Mobile2win SMS platform as an elegant solution to solicit contestant entries. 'Landline telephones are dead, and SMS is the new frictionless consumer response mechanic' was my pitch. Unfortunately, the mighty success of the KBC show had overwhelmed the senior management at Star India. They saw nothing defective with the old-fashioned dial-in mechanism and I was unceremoniously shooed away from their offices.

Just as Hindustan Lever had paved the way for me to become successful with contests2win.com, I intuitively knew that I needed a marquee television channel of India to be my partner for Mobile2win. If I managed to strike a deal with a large TV channel, everyone else in media would partner with us. And if we got media partners, the most prominent brands in the country would come rushing to us. The business credo I was working with was simple: brands loved consumers, consumers loved content and content loved media! If Mobile2win could enhance the engagement between audiences and content, media owners would make us lifetime partners, and that would make us very valuable.

After my rejection by Star India, I set my eyes on Sony Entertainment Television (SET) which was the number two TV channel in the country. I connected with them and actively began engaging with their management team. Our pitch to them was simple. Rajiv and I explained how we had leveraged the power of mobile phones with television in China by highlighting the key insight that consumers in India (like in China) were increasingly watching TV programmes with their mobile phones beside them. A fun, attractive, interactive mobile offering could engage passive TV viewers and motivate them to interact through SMS messages from their phones. SMS was a chargeable mobile service, and it would generate revenues for the TV channel, besides engaging its viewers.

In my entrepreneurial life, I have noticed that when there is an innovative, experimental and ambitious leader at the helm of the business, plenty of partnership possibilities open up. The day I met Sunil Lulla who was the head of SET, I knew I had found my ideal partner. Sunil loved new ideas, and he seemed very intrigued by the mobile ideas we presented to him.

At that time, Sony Entertainment's big new show was

a fun soap opera called 'Jassi Jassi Koi Nahi' (the story of an ignored office girl who becomes a corporate high-achiever). The title song of the show was very catchy, and I impulsively recorded it on my Nokia phone while watching the programme. Later, in the office, I got my technical team to convert the song into a ringtone. I had an excellent idea for SET that I wanted to showcase!

I requested a meeting with Sunil in his office, and went across to meet him along with two of my colleagues. I had pre-planned this pitch carefully and had our colleagues in our office on standby. Just as the three of us walked into Sunil's cabin in the Sony India office, I messaged my colleagues back in our office. A few minutes later, while we were sitting with Sunil, our office colleagues began calling each of us on our mobile phones that had been preloaded with the 'Jassi Jaisi Koi Nahi' ringtone. Almost like an orchestra, our mobile phones began playing the show tune at the exact same time! Sunil heard the ringtones and was stunned. As we placed our ringing phones on the table, Sunil became visibly excited and asked me what he could do with this idea. I had my plans ready and explained that all SET needed to do was to promote the ringtone via promotional ads on TV that would appear when 'Jassi Jaisi Koi Nahi' was being telecast. The ads would offer a unique 'Jassi Jaisi Koi Nahi' mobile ringtone exclusively to SET viewers, with simple instructions to download that ringtone for a small price. Mobile2win India would power the campaign with its shortcode and manage the entire backend, with cooperation from all the major mobile networks in India.

Sunil liked the idea, and we both shook hands on the spot agreeing to a fifty-fifty share on ringtone revenues. My first big Mobile2win India deal was done!

The next day I rushed to the offices of Vodafone and Airtel and began meeting their top honchos who handled the SMS and VAS (Value Added Services) business. Over time, Shailesh Varudkar at Vodafone and Mohit Bhatnagar (then at Airtel, now the Managing Director of Sequoia Capital) became good friends. I explained the unique innovation to them, and they were excited by the pioneering business model that promised to be very lucrative for all parties, especially as we reached scale. Both Airtel and Vodafone agreed to a fifty-fifty revenue share between Mobile2win and themselves. This finally meant that for every Rs 100 generated via the Jassi ringtone, Rs 50 would be kept by the operator and Rs 50 by Mobile2win. Of that Rs 50, Mobile2win would then share Rs 25 with Sony Entertainment Channel. This meant that our profit was Rs 25 for every Rs 100 generated. A 25 per cent margin for Mobile2win was not bad at all, especially when we were not making any significant investments in the business other than using our proprietary technology platform! I was convinced this was going to be a big win for me!

In our initial business estimates, both SET and Mobile2win India had estimated that a few thousand television users would pay to download the 'Jassi Jaisi Koi Nahi' ringtone. After the ringtone campaign went live, lakhs of viewers downloaded the ringtone. SET and Mobile2win had not only magically entertained viewers but had also created sizeable revenues with terrific profit margins from thin air! This was such a great example of 'creative technology' and was exactly the kind of business I wanted to be associated with. I had first caught a glimpse of this when I had gone to Italy to get trained on socks knitting machines. This time around, I felt so proud and grateful to be driving such a fantastic initiative myself!

Our relationship with SET and other media companies now developed a strong momentum. Rajiv Hiranandani, a perfect 'people's person' worked very hard and developed excellent relationships with all the telecom companies and their VAS teams. A few months later, we secured our very own SMS short code—8558—for India. It was terrific to have the same 8558 shortcodes operate both in India and China. With our shortcode in hand, we now began approaching top brands to run contests, promotions and lead management ideas with this simple SMS response mechanism. Just as I had asked brands to promote the contests2win.com link in their advertising communication when I launched contests2win.com, this time around we began asking the same brands to support the 8558 shortcodes in their television and print media ads. It was a virtuous circle that kept turning around every time technology leaped forward!

One evening, while returning home from the airport, I noticed many empty hoardings dotting the Mumbai skylines. All of them had more or less the same message—'Call X number for this hoarding'. These billboards came alive only at certain times and during the slow periods when brand campaigns had run dry, hoarding owners solicited business inquiries through this communication on their unsold hoardings.

When I observed these messages, I noticed an anomaly. For instance, if I was at Mahim, how could I identify the exact hoarding that I was interested in renting amongst the four or five hoardings available in that area? There was no distinct way to distinguish one hoarding from another. (In those days, mobile phones had very poor quality cameras, hence clicking pictures did not work). I was once again inspired and came up with a killer idea!

The next day, I contacted leading hoarding companies and pitched them my solution. Could they add a distinct code we would give them and paint them on each hoarding—such as 'SMS 01 to 8558' on hoarding 1; 'SMS 02 to 8558' on hoarding 2 and so on and so forth? My idea was to tag each hoarding with its unique code and have the hoarding company receive leads pointing to specific hoardings, to help them close deals quickly! One of the biggest hoarding agencies in Mumbai loved my idea and painted 8558 all over town with our unique codes. What I wanted to do was to get Mobile2win's 8558 shortcodes advertised free of cost, so that it could be seen everywhere by top brands and media companies. The empty hoardings painted with our shortcode, all over Mumbai fulfilled my goal magnificently. It was a win-win for the hoarding company too as it provided them with information on the exact hoarding that their customers were interested in.

MY LEARNINGS

The successful launch of Mobile2win India taught me many valuable lessons. The first one was that it was important to have a clearly identified business goal especially when starting up. I wanted to partner with a large TV channel for strategic reasons and I accomplished it. I firmly believe that from time to time, an entrepreneur must focus his energies on a single 'laser-targeted' task and work positively towards achieving it, with a premeditated mindset of victory. In my experience, when you wish for something and work hard at it, you will achieve it.

The second lesson I learned was to be open to the idea of finding like-minded co-founders and partners who were committed to making a startup business successful. I found Rajiv and Ranga who were rare professionals with a solid entrepreneurial streak in them.

Then comes the need to be 'street-smart' whenever the situation permitted. My trick of impressing Sunil Lulla with the Jassi ringtone taught me how important it was to demonstrate great ideas instead of just talking about them. It is imperative for an entrepreneur to develop his unique marketing and presentation panache and deliver it in his unique style. One has to work hard at this, but it is extremely important.

My success with the Mumbai hoardings taught me that any industry or process could be reinvented and disrupted with creative and innovative energy. Above all, I learnt that when an entrepreneur created ideas that were inherently helpful and delightful, the world would welcome him with open arms!

The Magic of 'Indian Idol'

After our early success with the 'Jassi Jaisi Koi Nahin' ringtone, Mobile2win India began to staff up and began doing roaring business with brands and media companies. One afternoon, I received a call from the Sony Entertainment Television (SET) office with a request to visit them for a business briefing. I chuckled even as I accepted the invite. In the initial stages of a startup, entrepreneurs don't need invitations to come to business meetings! We are so used to gatecrashing, and relentlessly cold-calling customers, any excuse to meet a client is great news!

At the meeting the next day, Sunil Lulla (the Executive Vice President of SET) asked me to take an oath of secrecy before divulging any more information to me. In typical Bollywood style, I swore on my business never to reveal what I was about to hear. Sunil took a deep breath in and shared that SET was partnering with the famous 'American Idol' TV show to launch the first-ever 'Indian Idol' show for the Indian television market. Sunil and his team seemed very excited and enthusiastic about this TV programme and were beaming from ear to ear. To be honest, I had not heard of 'American Idol'. It sounded like a very American show, which I intuitively felt would not find much appeal in India. But given the infectious enthusiasm around me, I nodded vigorously and pretended to be excited. Sunil asked me to think of all the interactive possibilities around the show and revert to him when I had all my ideas firmed up.

Back in the office, my team and I did plenty of research

on the American Idol show and understood its style and format. The US had an amazing talent pool of singers and stage performers, and I quickly understood why the show had become so popular there. I also learned that for American Idol, active audience participation by way of votes played a critical role in deciding the winners of the contest. SMS and mobile phone engagement were still not very popular in the US back then; their voting mechanisms were based on consumers calling landlines or logging into the official websites to cast their votes.

For us at Mobile2win, the answer and solution were obvious! We would offer the most robust SMS voting platform in the world to power up the Indian Idol competition and make this audience voting mechanism the 'coolest', simplest and most profitable way to engage and participate in the show! My team prepared a detailed proposal and sent it to Sunil and his team.

A few weeks later, I received a request once again to be present at the SET office for a 'crucial' meeting. This time, I was asked to come alone.

At the SET office, I was taken aback when I was led into a very large boardroom. Inside, I saw the Indian and foreign representatives of Sony, Freemantle (the global producer of 'American Idol') and from a few other agencies connected with the Indian Idol show. We were all seated at a long table with tall chairs. Sunil introduced me as the interactive media partner of SET and described the work we had done together with 'Jassi Jaisi Koi Nahi'. He shared how Mobile2win had created a new revenue line for SET through consumer-friendly, mobile content activation. Sunil then shared the Mobile2win proposal we had sent him that detailed the creation of a robust SMS voting platform for the 'Indian Idol' show. He clarified that while voting via landline calls would continue, voting by SMS would be the big, unique innovation SET would bring to this epic show. Mobile2win had proposed a 'premium' rate of Rs 3 per SMS for voting via SMS for 'Indian Idol' (The standard price for SMS at that time was Re 1). I had even secured a nod from some mobile operators to activate this campaign (I had not revealed to them that it was for 'Indian Idol').

After listening to my introduction and proposal, a tall American gentleman asked me, 'Mr Kejriwal, we have heard some good things about your capabilities and innovations. Tell me, how many SMS votes do you think you will be able to attract for the "Indian Idol"?'

That question was a total googly for me. I had no idea about SET's projected reach (the number of viewers who would watch) for this show. Without that number, it was difficult to calculate how many SET viewers would spend Rs 3 per SMS votes to passively vote in a brand new TV show. I also found it hard to understand why viewers of this show would spend their hard-earned money to vote for young, unknown boys and girls, who would be singing and dancing on a TV screen when they (the viewers) had grown up admiring Bollywood stars. I was baffled and couldn't immediately come up with an answer.

A long pause later, just as I was about to say something, Sunil interrupted me in Hindi and said 'Boss, *Hindi mein pehle tera number mujhe bataa. Nahin toh sab ki reputation barbaad kar degaa!'* (Boss, first tell me your number in Hindi or else you will ruin all our reputations!) I switched to Hindi and said, 'Sunil, I'm guessing ten thousand votes?

That's about the number of contest responses we get for TV-sponsored campaigns on contests2win.com. Since this will be a premium, paid mobile SMS service, I think it will be the same number, despite the large visibility of the show.' Sunil heard me but didn't seem pleased with my estimate. But, he couldn't figure out a number himself and so asked me to go ahead and make my claim.

I looked confidently at the American gentleman and said, 'Sir, we will get ten thousand SMS votes for the "Indian Idol" contest.' I pronounced 'thousand' as 'thouzzzzand' to make it sound grand. The American stared at me as if he had seen a ghost. His face turned pale and he said, 'Alok, do you have any clue what American Idol is? More Americans vote for their "American Idol" than they vote for their President.'

I kept my composure and slowly replied, 'Sir, I have all the respect for your show and its popularity. However, in India, it's a new idea and has a cost attached to it. I'm just being conservative.' The American turned away from me, looked at his colleagues and shrugged his shoulders. I think he felt like throwing me out of the room.

The meeting concluded a few minutes later, and the Chief Technology Officer of SET, Mr Anil Garg (also present in the meeting) was requested by Sunil to audit Mobile2win technology and its backend systems.

A week later, we were back at the SET office and walked Anil through our entire tech platform and its backend. Anil was a technology veteran and asked us many hard questions. There were no internet 'cloud' services back then, and we had to convince him that we would be able to make the large investments in servers to manage a show that would run just for a few hours in a week. After a gruelling session, we won Anil's favour and were greenlighted to be the official SMS partner for the Indian Idol contest. The only one condition SET placed on us was that we needed to acquire a dedicated shortcode for them instead of using our own Mobile2win's 8558 code. Our COO, Rajiv Hiranandani worked hard and procured the shortcode 2525 for SET.

A few weeks later, SET launched the 'Indian Idol' show and the moment the SMS voting contest was announced on the show, our servers were flooded with SMS responses. We had underestimated the messages we would receive in a very short window of time. Many of the SMSes began to fail because of our technology backend. The problem was not hard to figure out. We owned an inadequate numbers of servers to handle the high spike of incoming SMS messages. The burden of owning more servers would have cost Mobile2win many lakhs of rupees and would have made no business sense. The show was a weekly one, and we couldn't have bought an abnormally large number of servers just to be used for one hour a week! Instead of profits, we would have been saddled with massive losses.

One desperate evening, during the live telecast of the show, I was in the Mobile2win office chewing my nails as I saw the SMS responses ramp up and hit peak load. Almost instantly, the service began to crash, and voters who were voting for the show started to see the dreadful 'message not sent' alert on their phones. I was very anxious and said aloud, 'Is there anyone in the office who has an idea to make this smoother? Any suggestions?'

After a moment of silence, I saw a hand go up from behind a pillar in the office. The person who wanted to speak was Sachin Jain—a young engineer who had joined us only a few weeks ago. He must have been barely twenty-two or twenty-three at that time. I did not know his name, and in an irritated voice said, 'Yes boss, tell me what's your idea?'

Sachin stood up and very gently said, 'Alok Sir, when viewers send messages to vote for Indian Idol, do they need to get a "read receipt" back for their SMSs?' (Those who may remember SMS services of feature phones might recall that there was an optional service that returned a 'receipt' to the sender of a message indicating that the receiver had received the message.)

I was puzzled and said, 'Why do you ask this?'

Sachin replied, 'Because for every SMS vote we get, we have to send read receipts back to the voters. That creates a massive reverse traffic load on our servers and causes a choke.'

I immediately got the point he was making and excitedly told him, 'No one cares about receiving a "read receipt" when voting for "Indian Idol"! Kill the receipt messaging. Now!'

Sachin switched off the read receipt system and like magic, the servers lit up beautifully and managed to handle the load of the show that day! A brilliant, young engineer had saved the soon-to-be mighty "Indian Idol", SET, and Mobile2win from failing badly!

By the time the first season had ended, the 'Indian Idol' show was a super hit and a massive success for SET. The show introduced the genre of reality entertainment television in India and was a big, big win for me and Mobile2win India!

Now to go back to the question that the American

gentleman had asked me in the SET office about the number of votes I would be able to get for the 'Indian Idol' show to which I had bravely replied that we would receive ten thousand votes.

Before reading further, I would urge you to pause for a moment and think of a number in your mind and then continue reading.

When the final numbers were tallied, the total votes cast by SMS exceeded one crore votes (over ten million!). My original prediction was a sad, miserly, one-hundredth of this number.

MY LEARNINGS

There were so many lessons I learned from the success of 'Indian Idol'. The first one was never to underestimate success. As an entrepreneur, I had become so adept at facing rejections, defeats and multiple failures that any unprecedented success seemed to appear like a fairy tale to me. The Indian Idol show proved to me that good fortune awaited the entrepreneur who executed on his vision.

Young Sachin Jain taught me what I refer to as the 'creativity of naivety'. The concept is simple: when your mind is pure and not clouded by any preconceived notions, you have amazing clarity and breakthrough ideas emerge. Sunil Lulla's outstanding leadership and ability to take a massive risk with Mobile2win taught me how great

leaders help make big ideas become a reality. He
also demonstrated to me that cultivating partners
and trusting them was vital and crucial to creating
long-term value in a business.

Staying Firm

A few episodes after the massive success of the 'Indian Idol' show for which my startup Mobile2win had deployed an SMS voting platform, my team met me for a debriefing session. They updated me on the status of the telecom networks they had signed up in India that were connected to our SMS platform. Since the platform was built for a new shortcode 2525 dedicated to Sony Entertainment Television (SET), we needed to sign up all the popular mobile telecom companies in India so that consumers of those networks could seamlessly vote for the Indian Idol contest via premium SMS.

Rajiv Hiranandani, the CEO of Mobile2win India told me that all the networks in India had signed up except for BSNL (Bharat Sanchar Nigam Limited). Despite many requests from our side as well as from SET, BSNL had not responded. We were puzzled why BSNL was keeping away from a deal that could potentially generate massive revenues for them, given the enormous number of votes being cast for each Indian Idol episode via premium SMS.

I took it upon myself to find the roadblock and booked a flight to Delhi to meet key BSNL personnel. Their building near Connaught Place was imposing, and the only office I have ever visited that had a column in the visitors' register for 'Firearms and Ammunition'. I still haven't been able to figure out why people with weapons would visit BSNL...

I was three minutes before time and was seated in a conference room that seemed to have been furnished in the 1970s. The officials of BSNL were late for their meeting with me, and their common secretary kept darting in and out of the conference room making excuses about why the team members had still not arrived. I was prepared for such delays that were typical of government meetings.

Forty minutes later, many men stormed into the room. They all seemed to be senior officials of BSNL, and when they handed me their cards, I knew they were the decision-makers I needed to impress to get BSNL to sign up for 'Indian Idol'.

The seniormost officer greeted me warmly and said, 'Kejriwalji, the Sony Television programme of "Indian Idol" is very good! My children like the singers.' All the other men in the room solemnly agreed with Mr Senior Officer. Then the man said, 'Tell me, who will win? My children keep asking me, and I thought I would ask you.'

I gently replied and said, 'Sir, this is not a pre-fixed reality show! As the singers perform and present themselves, the audience and the judges try and select the best amongst them. The rest get eliminated automatically. Please communicate the same to your kids and ask them to keep voting.' I said that deliberately because I assumed that this officer's kids would own BSNL powered mobile phones that would not be able to vote through SMS due to our unsigned agreement. I was fishing to check how vulnerable the officer was.

The senior officer grunted an acknowledgment that sounded more like disbelief.

I said, 'Sir, we have an excellent response to the show, and SMS is the overwhelming choice of consumers to cast their votes. We have signed up all the mobile networks in India and want to make sure that BSNL also benefits from the show. I am told that the agreement we sent to you many weeks ago is still held up. How can I help to close out the deal?'

The officer looked at me, smiled and said, 'Yes, Kejriwalji, I agree. The show is a hit. Lots of my office people have been telling me also to get the deal signed. But I hope you realise that we are BSNL and given the special status we have as a government mobile network, we would like a better revenue share than the one you have proposed in the agreement you have sent to us.'

Finally, I figured what was holding up the agreement!

I waited for a few seconds and replied, 'Sir, this is the same revenue share we have signed across all operators. As the mobile partner of Sony TV, we have come to this revenue share number with utmost fairness. Also, a few percentage points should not be the matter of discussion; what we should be doing as partners is growing the audience that participates via SMS votes so that more revenue is generated for both of us.'

I spoke like a well-groomed, polite, startup CEO talking with all the humility I could offer to close out a deal.

The senior officer seemed obstinate and said, 'No, Mr Kejriwal. We need a higher percentage, or we won't sign. I know we are losing revenue, but we cannot be treated like other mobile network operator.'

While on the flight to Delhi, I had rehearsed this meeting repeatedly in my mind. I tried to remember my earlier interactions with government agencies. My job in my Nana's transport company that involved dealing with ONGC (another large government enterprise) flashed before me. I knew how impractical and egotistical government officers could be. To beat BSNL, I needed a trump card. After a lot of brain-wracking, I had discovered one!

Back in the ancient BSNL meeting room, I pushed my chair slightly backward as if I was getting ready to leave. Then, I looked at the officer and said, 'Sure Sir, I understand. Since we cannot give you more revenue share, we will not be able to work with you. To do justice to the millions of viewers watching the show, Sony Television will start adding a message on the voting instructions flashed during the Indian Idol show that will advise viewers that they will be able to vote on all mobile networks in India except BSNL. We will mention that BSNL is not our voting partner. I know BSNL consumers will be disappointed, but we will need to be truthful to them.' After saying this, I politely got up, shook hands with all the officers and walked out of the room.

The next day when I had barely settled into my office chair, I got a message from Rajiv Hiranandani. He said, 'The BSNL guys have signed the agreement and couriered it to us. Thanks, Alok.'

MY LEARNINGS

This incident is one of my favourites and makes me proud of my salesmanship. In this particular case, instead of begging and pleading with a demanding customer or yielding to his demands to get him to accept my offer, I said, 'No. Not interested. I will not bow or bend to accommodate your unreasonable demand.'

I have learned that for a successful sales person, sacrificing profit margins, underselling, competing blindly (often to prevent someone else from getting an order) should never be an option. You must boldly say 'not interested' and move on. Trust me, if your product or service is valuable and will add value to your customer, they will call you back. Finally, in the rare cases, where you need to act tough, you should act tough and get your deal done. It's all good karma when it comes to sales.

I Get Fired. I Get Rich!

Mobile2win India was the first mover in the value-added services space in India, and with the Indian Idol partnership, we were undoubtedly at the top of the game. As the 'Indian' Idol show ramped up and became one of the most successful television shows in India, Mobile2win became *the* brand to reckon with when it came to mobile engagement and interactive services.

Rajiv Hiranandani, the COO of Mobile2win India had expanded his team and moved into a larger office in the same building where I operated contests2win.com. His sales and business team had signed up most of the top brands in India and were executing multiple campaigns for them. Mobile2win ventured into mobile content such as wallpapers and ringtones, and I had helped them sign on iconic brands such as Sholay and Tarla Dalal to create games and applications. Mobile2win had also found a market in the Middle East and had begun working with Omantel in Oman for building a large content platform for their consumer services. Sony Entertainment Television (SET) had made Mobile2win their long-term mobile activation partner, and with their slew of TV shows, plenty of new content got added to the suite of offerings we could offer as Value Added Services (VAS) to mobile consumers in India.

The success of Mobile2win India was ironically throwing up another problem. Since the company had massively ramped up its business, there was a significant increase in overheads, salaries, and operating costs. Mobile2win

India needed a series B investment. Unfortunately, the existing investors in the company—Siemens Mobile Acceleration from Munich, Softbank Ventures from China and contests2win India were unable to invest additional money in the company. Siemens Mobile and Softbank China were based outside of India and did not invest in Indian startups. Mobile2win India was a dedicated India-focussed business. In fact, both Siemens and Softbank wanted to exit the India business. My company, contests2win.com had just turned profitable, and we were in no position to invest considerable amounts of money in Mobile2win India either.

A trickier problem was that the existing investors were not on good terms with Gopala Krishna (GK) who had returned to India to run Mobile2win India as CEO.

I was fortunate to have built up strong relationships with many VCs in India who respected me as a pioneering internet entrepreneur and a survivor of the dot-com bust. I leveraged all my connections and began pitching the Mobile2win India deal with the investors I knew. Along with my business plan, I also mentioned that the existing investors, Softbank and Siemens wanted to exit from the company. Amongst the many investors I met, Sandeep Singhal of Sequoia India (that later became Westbridge) showed lots of interest and stayed up late one night in his room at the Taj Mumbai to deliver a term sheet to me. I needed it urgently to present it to the Mobile2win board meeting in Mumbai the next day. Sandeep's deal promised to invest adequately in Mobile2win, but he was not prepared to buy out Softbank and Siemens Mobile. That deal fell through.

As I met many more VCs, my mission to close a financing

round for Mobile2win India began to look very tough. VCs were not interested in making other VCs rich (at least in the case of Mobile2win India). Ours was a young, new venture and incoming VCs felt that the earlier investors of Mobile2win India needed to stay invested in the business as proof of their belief in the model and potential of the company. Many VCs offered plenty of money to fund Mobile2win India as new capital but none for Softbank and Siemens Mobile to exit. This deal began looking like a difficult one for me to close.

One afternoon, I met Pramod Haque and Vab Goel of Norwest Venture Partners. Vab Goel dramatically introduced Pramod Haque to me as the 'investor with the Midas touch' and showed me pictures of him featured on prominent magazine covers. I had heard of Pramod Haque before and felt honoured that he was sitting across me in my office discussing Mobile2win India.

A few minutes into the meeting, I messaged GK to come in and join us. I introduced him to Pramod and Vab as the CEO of Mobile2win India. I wanted to make sure I projected myself as an investor of Mobile2win India with little involvement in day-to-day management. After I exited the conference room, GK spent a couple of hours going over the entire business with them.

A week later, Norwest came back to meet us again, accompanied by Sandeep Singhal of Nexus Venture Partners (There are two Sandeep Singhals in the Indian VC world). I knew Sandeep Singhal well since he had been the third partner of Neeraj Bhargava and Rajesh Jog of eVentures that had invested in contests2win.com. Sandeep had lived in the US for many years, and while he was not actively involved with contests2win.com, we were in regular touch. He had also become the caretaker of eVentures after the fund shut down in India and regularly received my contests2win. com board updates. Sandeep had just launched his new VC firm—Nexus Venture Partners and Mobile2win India looked like becoming their first deal.

In the discussions that followed, I got a strong sense that Norwest and Nexus clearly understood the opportunities and challenges of investing in Mobile2win India. Sandeep had known me for years and had seen our growth and consistency at contests2win.com and the successful launch and exit of Mobile2win China. Over the next few days, Vab from Norwest became the active driver of the investment discussions and began speaking with Siemens and Softbank in China to understand their exit valuation expectations. Parallelly, he engaged with the Mobile2win management led by GK and Rajiv, and also spoke to the business partners and clients of Mobile2win India. I remained detached from the day-to-day calls, questions, and clarifications that Norwest kept sending the Mobile2win India management team. I innocently assumed I was being respected as the founder and as the early investor of Mobile2win India.

A few days later, late in the afternoon, I received a phone call that precipitated one of the most difficult, gut-wrenching and traumatic episodes of my life.

Vab from Norwest Venture Partners was on the phone and informed me that he had settled all the exit issues of Softbank and Siemens Mobile by offering them cash for their stakes at a very attractive valuation. Vab mentioned that he was also prepared a large tranche of money to be invested into Mobile2win India as a fresh investment to help develop the business, and had aligned GK and Rajiv with his vision for scaling Mobile2win India. The new investors led by Norwest and Nexus had carved out an extensive ESOP (Equity Share Options Plan) for the existing employees of the Company, and everyone in the team was very excited.

Vab suddenly stopped speaking. I could still hear his breathing on the other side. My heart started pounding, and I burst out saying, 'Wow, Vab, you've cracked this deal! Everything sounds awesome. I look forward to ...'

Vab interrupted me (that was his typical style) and said, 'Alok, we are all set, but we have one condition that we need to fulfill. And for that, I need your complete cooperation.'

I excitedly said, 'Shoot Vab ... tell me what I can do, to get this done?'

Vab slowly said, 'Alok, we want you out of the company. You need to exit Mobile2win India.'

When I heard those words, I immediately assumed he meant that I needed to distance myself from the day-to-day management and let GK and Rajiv run the business with complete independence. I replied, 'Vab, I don't play an executive role in the business. I barely know what's going on on a day-to-day basis. I only help crack top level deals and help with strategy ...'

Vab interrupted me again and said, 'That's exactly my point. Since you don't have a management role to play, you are just an investor without any money. We need you to go out with Softbank and Siemens Mobile. As an entrepreneur-promoter, you will never have enough money to invest in the company, and we need to free up your equity to make room for more investors and employees. We propose to pay you the same handsome price we are paying Siemens and Softbank and completely buy you out.'

Before I could react further, Vab continued speaking and said, 'Alok, in my life as a VC, I have rarely seen entrepreneur-founders get rich. You are going to be a multi-millionaire in a short period. The money that comes into your hands can be used to do so much more. You're a smart guy and will go far.'

I was stunned. Instantly, I understood the mutiny that had been hatched. Vab had convinced GK and Rajiv that they no longer needed me to be a part of their team, and with Norwest and Nexus backing them, there was no reason for me to stay on as a shareholder. My very own people had been turned against me. Norwest wanted to make the company entirely VC-managed, without my entrepreneurial DNA!

Over the ensuing weeks, I understood that this was a non-negotiable stance by Norwest. Siemens and Softbank, the other two investors of Mobile2win India, were thrilled with the terms they had received and began to pressurise me to exit.

For those who may not be familiar with startups and their funding agreements, most entrepreneurs sign mountains of complex, draconian contracts when they raise money. Embedded inside these documents are deadly clauses, such as the one called the 'drag out' provision that allows the investors to literally drag out the founder-promoter in the event of a sale or change in management of the startup. In my particular case, it was this clause that was being invoked. I was being offered a very handsome sum of money to walk out of my own company forcibly.

The harsh reality of the situation began to sink in. Here I was—someone who had founded a great company that was wonderfully positioned in the perfect storm of the lucrative Mobile Value Added Services (MVAS) explosion in India. Just when my fortunes were about to start looking up, I was being forced to walk out of my own company with just a few million dollars. This was the greatest ironies of them all.

I reviewed the agreements I had signed with Siemens and Softbank while starting up Mobile2win India and realised that they were watertight and did not allow me any relief to refuse the sale of my shares by way of the drag out clause. While I could have just refused to sign and forced a legal case to be filed, that would have meant the complete ruin of Mobile2win India. The company was growing fast and would collapse if it was not immediately funded. Norwest had understood this predicament and planned its strategy accordingly.

I felt helpless and paralysed and turned to ICICI Ventures, my most supportive VC and guardian through the years for guidance. Bala Deshpande and Nandini Satam at ICICI were very supportive of me and also very objective while advising and mentoring me. They made me patiently understand the situation. They also promised to be on my side irrespective of whatever decision I took. They were my real God-sent angels. To this date, I regard ICICI Ventures as one of the best things that ever happened to me as an entrepreneur.

Three days later, sometime around 2 a.m. in the night, I woke up and walked into my living room. There, I brooded about my forced exit from Mobile2win. I would be rich and receive substantial cash to do many other things. At the same time, I would have to sign a three-year, non-compete agreement that would prevent me from doing anything with the mobile business, globally! The most painful part was that I would have to live without being a part of Mobile2win India—a business that I had started and which had the potential to become a billion-dollar company. But I knew I was helpless in this situation.

The next morning, I had made up my mind. I called Vab and said, 'I'm selling.'

The Mobile2win India deal was closed within four months. While I got rich, the money didn't seem to make any difference to me. The months that passed after signing and transferring of my shares were very dark and gloomy. The lucrative business of MVAS in India haunted me, and I often wondered if I had lost the most significant opportunities of my life. In the meanwhile, richly-funded Mobile2win India hired bigwigs from the entertainment and media industry and moved into a 10,000 square feet office (from the 1500 square feet office that I had rented for them). They hired over 200 new people and seemed to be the hottest company around.

Little did I know at that time that my coerced exit from Mobile2win was the second incredible divine intervention in my life.

Since I couldn't do anything with mobile phones for three years, I turned back to the internet and pondered about what I could do there? At home, my daughters were growing up fast, and they would fight for time on the family desktop computer to play online games on casual gaming websites. As I stared at them playing simple and casual games, it occurred to me that I was staring at the future! The internet browser was becoming ubiquitous across the world, and kids were enjoying playing quick web games instead of playing console games that needed an elaborate set up with extra hardware. I saw the mouse replacing the joystick. Also, I had never seen girls play online games with the kind of passion with which my girls were playing them. So far, I had only seen boys played racing cars and shooting games, tummy-down in the living room on their consoles.

A few days later, in the winter of 2006, I decided to start my new venture—games2win.com—that would focus on online, casual, fun games for girls. I was on to my third startup.

Now, if you are wondering about Mobile2win India, this is what happened:

In less than twelve months after the sale of my shares, dangerous cracks began to appear in the MVAS business in India. Mobile operators began to understand the power of MVAS content, the potential of revenue it could generate from their consumers and started to renegotiate deals they had signed with intermediaries of the likes of Mobile2win. The 50 per cent revenue share I had signed up with mobile operators came crashing down to less than 25 per cent. On the media side, TV channels such as SET began to realise that it was their media that drove mobile responses and engagement. They started demanding more revenue share from their partners. The 50 per cent that I had signed with SET collapsed to a bare 15-20 per cent.

MVAS companies began getting treated like 'dalals' (brokers/middlemen) and got hit from both sides—their content partners and the mobile operators. The margins in the business began eroding fast, while the costs of employees and operating costs continued to rise. Also, the revenue share payments from mobile operators that would originally arrive in a couple of months began to get severely delayed and would be paid out with unexplainable deductions ascribed to 'reconciliation errors'. MVAS companies like Mobile2win had neither leverage nor method to combat these deductions with the mobile operators or to negotiate better terms with them.

The MVAS business model of being an intermediary between content provider, mobile operator and consumer that seemed to have been such a golden opportunity just a year earlier, now seemed doomed. Some of the top executives hired by Norwest at Mobile2win India were asked to move on. GK was let go of. Twenty-four months later as the company derailed further, it was sold for a cashless exchange of shares to a Chandigarh MVAS company called Altruist. The sale was a sign that the Mobile2win India business had collapsed and had been parcelled away in a deal that was meant to save face for the investors.

It became evident that the forced acquisition of my Mobile2win India stake was the best thing that had happened to me. It allowed me to profitably exit a toxic business and helped me start Games2win—my best venture to date!

MY LEARNINGS

I learned that VCs could destroy and wreck a great startup if left uncontrolled. Mobile2win India might have declined in profitability but would not have been sold at a throwaway price if the VCs had retained some entrepreneur DNA in it. The incident taught me about people and their motivations. I learned that it was not fair on my part to expect loyalty forever. This deal also educated me a lot more about VCs and investors. Many of them did not understand the day-to-day, granular details of running a business and assumed that a business model was just an excel sheet that could be projected to grow by formulae extrapolated into months and years. This story also made me experience personally a famous saying I had heard all my life: 'Whatever happens, happens for the good.'

REFLECTIONS

SELF-RESPECT ABOVE ALL

It was at the Shamiana, the old coffee shop of the Taj Mahal Hotel in Mumbai where I first told my family about my idea for creating a website called contests2win.com. My two sisters, one of my brothers-in-law, my wife Chhavi and I were snacking there. When things became a little quiet around me, I mentioned my venture as if it were a prophetic announcement. No one at the table reacted. They kept talking amongst themselves. I cleared my throat and repeated myself, this time a bit loudly. Chhavi looked at me, smiled and then burst out laughing! My sisters immediately caught on and began giggling together. All of them either thought I was joking or that the name contests2win.com sounded funny. Either way, they ignored me and quickly became absorbed in the other conversations at the table. I felt a bit hurt and surprised by their reactions, but didn't pay too much attention to their dismissal.

A few months later, after I had launched contests2win. com, I began calling as many customers as I could for business. The Godrej group was on top of my list. I called the Godrej landline and was connected to a lady who was in charge of marketing soaps and deodorants. After we had exchanged greetings, I slowly explained who I was and said, 'My name is Alok, and I am the founder of contests2win.com.'

The lady interrupted me and asked me, 'Sorry, where are you calling from?' I said, 'From contests2win.com'.

She replied, 'Is that ... errr ... the name of your company?'

I said, 'Yes Ma'am, my company is called contests2win. com.'

I heard the lady cover her telephone mouthpiece, chuckle

a couple of times and loudly tell colleagues around her, 'Gosh! There is a fellow on the line who owns a company called contests2win.com. How stupid is that!' When she came back on the call, she said she would 'let me know'. I never got any direct business from her or the Godrej group.

When I heard that lady laugh at my company name, I was upset. Was the name of my startup so stupid and funny that it had my immediate family and now a top potential client laughing at it? The thought irked me for a few minutes, but I cast it aside. I was confident that I had a strong idea, even if its name sounded funny.

As destiny would have it, just a few months later, when MTV India actively began working with contests2win.com, the first contest that we powered up together was a really funny Godrej Cinthol contest called 'Baas Baby Baas' ('Baas' is smell in Hindi, and the Cinthol brand was promoting its new deodorant through this contest). I did a lot of business with the Godrej group after that.

As salespeople, we meet all kinds of buyers. Many tough ones; some who are challenging to manage and service; a few who are plain confused; a minority who think they own you just because they have given business to you and of course, plenty who are professional and courteous. Take for instance the famous Indian writer and author Amish Tripathi. Way before Amish became the renowned writer that he is today, he worked as a banker in financial services and was my client at IDBI Bank at Cuffe Parade and later at DBS Bank in Fort Mumbai. Amish did a series of promotions with us at contests2win.com and he was one of the most detailed, meticulous and precise clients we have ever had. Each of Amish's briefs was so well-written and and detail-oriented, that it became the 'template' we used to send to our other clients for their briefs. Clients like Amish taught us *how to do business* beyond just giving us business.

Within this eclectic mix of customers, there is also a chance you will meet a kind of sadistic buyer—someone who gets pleasure from troubling you, without any intention of actually doing business. If that sounds hard to believe, read on.

I met one such client in a multinational paints company in Gurgaon. This man would keep accepting my meeting requests and ask me to come to meet him in his office. There, he would keep me waiting for hours and later send me a message with the operator that he had become busy or that his boss had called him for an urgent meeting, etc. He did this with me three or four times. Nevertheless, I was relentless and kept visiting him. One day, after he had called me and made me wait for about forty minutes, he came to meet me personally and informed me that there was no vacant meeting room for us to meet! The multinational he worked in had a sprawling office, and I was sure this was just another trick of his, to torment me by calling me to his office and then asking me to leave.

The lobby area I was sitting in was full of visitors, and when he mentioned that there was no meeting room available, I raised my voice slightly and said, 'Sir, there is a room available! May I suggest it?' This man looked at me perplexed, gulped and said, 'Hmmm ... I'm not sure. Tell me, which room is available?' I looked at him while others in the waiting room were carefully listening in and said, 'Sir, the men's toilet. There is a space for my laptop near the washbasins, and all I need is a few minutes. Can we go there together?'

The man's face turned ashen and immediately apologetic. He had realised that his sadistic game was up. He said, 'No need, Alok. Give me a few minutes.' Five minutes later, I was sitting in the most gorgeous boardroom I have ever seen. The man was polite, repentant and gave me a good, substantial order!

MY LEARNINGS

As a seller, I have learned that come what may, I will never lose or compromise my self-respect for anything, leave alone a business deal. Losing dignity means stooping below the threshold of purpose, intent, and effort. As a salesperson, your pride in your work should come shining through. No matter if people laugh or try and play tricks on you, you must hold your chin up high, smile and keep striving. In the case of folks who just want to have fun with you, you must politely set them right. Having said this, a great salesperson always keeps his ego aside when doing deals. Sales and Ego never go well together.

REFLECTIONS
TWO PERSONAL CONVERSATIONS

In conclusion, I feel compelled to share two short stories which define my core understanding of entrepreneurship. They help to centre me whenever I feel out of balance.

Buy a big new car

A few weeks after I launched contests2win.com I realised I needed a privacy policy and a user agreement for my website. When I contacted my family lawyer D.H. Nanavati for help, he had no clue what a privacy policy meant, leave alone a detailed user agreement for a website. Mr Nanavati was kind enough to refer me to a young lawyer and said, 'Alok, if there is one chap in Mumbai who knows what the heck you are talking about, it is this fellow called Gautam Patel.' (Gautam Patel is now a very well-known and respected judge in the Mumbai High Court and on track to becoming one of India's biggest legal luminaries). I called Gautam Patel and explained the website concept to him. He said, 'Looks simple enough, Alok. Let's meet at the verandah of the Willingdon Club (Mumbai) and discuss this.'

The next day, over coffees and sandwiches, Gautam single-handedly wrote out a brand new customer privacy policy for me and added critical legal points to the user agreement. He used several thick Mont Blanc Ink pens to work with. When we were done, he relooked at the documents, then at me and said, 'Hmmm ... Alok, you seem to have an interesting idea in this contests site. The moment it picks up, and someone comes along to buy it, sell it, and buy yourself a big new car.'

'Buy a big new car' resonated in my mind when I left the Willingdon Club that day. Gautam had amusingly predicted that I was on the path of creating something valuable.

Contests2win.com was never sold. It made handsome profits and incubated new businesses such as Mobile2win, koimoi, and Games2win while creating significant value for all stakeholders. The sweet irony of this story is that contests2win.com bought me a 'big new car' in the July of this year, while quietly humming along and doing its business, without getting sold!

Gautam Patel had innocently wished me good luck and added a dollop of humour about the destiny of my startup. Neither of us could have predicted the extent of its success and the dividends I would earn from it. I learned that these unexpected and unplanned outcomes could keep struggling entrepreneurs motivated to keep going until they realise that it's the journey and not the destination that finally matters.

Time for me to stop wearing my socks

Unlike my Nana whom I grew up with, my father is a serious person. He speaks very little, focuses on discussing essential things and has unyielding views on many things. After working with him for years, I was ready to step out of his socks factory and start my new venture, contests2win.com. My concept was overwhelmingly strong, and I was convinced it would work. I was hesitant to inform my father about this decision of mine since I had no clue how he would take it. Would he just ignore my idea (like he usually did with ideas that didn't interest him), or just dismiss it with harsh words?

We were in my Dad's Cielo car and headed to Andheri (a suburb of Mumbai) to meet one of our C&A socks buyers when I decided to break the news to him. I said, 'Papa,

I'm thinking of doing something on my own, beyond the factory ...' My father smiled, looked at me intently and said, 'Sure... tell me what you are thinking?' I cleared my throat and very softly said, 'It's an internet idea to do contests and promotions of various brands on a website. Contests are very popular in India, and I want to create a single destination for them on the internet. My site is called contests2win.com.'

My Dad smiled again, looked at me lovingly and said, 'Of course, Alok. You must try this.' He hesitated for a while, looked away and then brought his gaze back to me. He said, 'All I want you to remember is that good ideas start just like this. You have to keep doing your best and keep at it. Just remember to be patient, because everything starts small.'

'Everything starts small' was the most prophetic blessing I had ever heard in my life. To this day, I thank my father for giving me the best advice I had ever received.

MY LEARNINGS

As an entrepreneur, I've learned that no one knows the power and destiny of an idea when it begins to get executed. Projections captured in Excel sheets, beautifully sculpted Powerpoint business plans and future roadmaps seem inconsequential when you look at them a few years later. Intriguingly, almost always, an entrepreneur underestimates the significant potential of his idea, the success and the accomplishment it may bring.

What I have learned well is that all that the entrepreneur must do is keep building his business hour by hour, day by day, year by year. When doing becomes more important than succeeding, everything falls into place. If you have the commitment, drive, and enthusiasm to pursue your dream, you will achieve super success. You just have to be diligent and patient and when you feel disheartened, just remember my Dad's message: 'All things start small.'

ENTERPRENEUR SPEAK
SALES—THE 'HOLY SCIENCE'

In my view, Sales is a 'Holy Science'. After all, it is the magic of sales that led me to create my startups, attract VC investments, hire people, woo customers and even find buyers for my businesses.

Sales, I believe, is the noblest of professions. It is what keeps a business going. Sales is 'the moment of truth' of any product or service. Most entrepreneurs know the universal law—no matter how great their product or service is, it is worth nothing until it sells. Also, sales may not always be for money. It is also about consumption—the ability to get people motivated to consume what you offer. As some of the most valuable companies in the world providing free services such Facebook, Google, and Dropbox have proven—if consumers love what you can offer them, and can't get enough of it, plenty of money flows in eventually.

I believe that everyone must acquire the skill to sell. This applies to entrepreneurs, businesspeople, professionals, homemakers, artists, students, everyone, anyone! If you're wondering why I am so enamoured by sales, read on. I have my reasons.

NOT THE FIRST OR SECOND, BUT THE THIRD SALE

The first sale usually happens if the seller is very passionate, determined, acquainted with the buyer, or offers her product or service for free. The second sale to the same customer is a tougher one. The seller needs to deeply establish a more in-depth 'why' for the buyer to buy again. Usually, the benefit of the first sale is examined and becomes the raison d'etre for a second sale. As a seller, if you try hard enough, you do get a second sale.

The third sale to the same customer is what I consider to be the 'real' sale. The third time, the buyer buys if there is real, tangible value in your product or service that is useful to him. Notice how the rule of the third sale applies to free things as well! So often we pass by people offering to hand out free flyers and pamphlets that you just don't care about because they are not valuable to you. The same is the case with 98 per cent of the free websites and mobile apps and games of the world. In the case of mobile games, after the first or second visit, almost 60 per cent consumers don't go back to the game because of the lack of tangible benefit (in this case, entertainment). The third time repeat sale is the real test of a seller, and if you do manage to create a product that repeatedly sells to the same buyer over and over again, you will have created a precious and profitable business. This is why Warren Buffett loves his investments in Coca-Cola and Gillette. If Coca-Cola and Gillette seem out of context, think of Skype, Uber, Amazon and Whatsapp and how often you use their services. These are amongst the most valuable companies in the world.

HOW DOES ONE LEARN THE ART OF SALES? WHAT WORKS AND WHAT DOESN'T?

These are some of the principles that have worked for me:

Absolute passion

I always tell people that their eyes should magically twinkle when they sell! Many of my clients have told me about my sparkling eyes when I have sold to them. The passion, the energy, your joy of offering your product or service should be so intense that the person on the other side feels your deep conviction and says, 'Done deal' without hesitation. This divine energy cannot be sprayed on like perfume. The seller must be so involved and in love with his product that he casts a spell on the buyer. I have seen this magic happen when entrepreneurs and inventors manage sales themselves instead of hiring professionals to sell on their behalf, especially in the early, formative stage of their businesses.

Being observant

I once saw a movie in which an investigator enters a room for less than thirty seconds, but in that short period of time, manages to observe everything inside, including the photos on the desk, the books on the shelves, posters and educational degrees hung on walls, and even what's inside the waste paper bin. He returns to his office and then notes down everything he saw in that room. Just like the investigator, I make it a practice to observe everything when I enter my buyer's office. This practice has worked well for me. From the education degrees hung on the wall, I deduce if my buyer has a vanity fetish. If yes, he will most likely buy a solution from me that will make him look smarter in the organisation over other people. I listen to how he speaks to his colleagues and his boss. If he is very subservient, he will not be able to take the final decision. If he is a bully, he will most probably give me a hard time and do his best to beat me down.

Once, I was sitting with a Director of a large multinational corporation when he received a call from his fourteen-year-old son. The man spent seven minutes coaxing the rebel teenager to have milk and food while keeping me waiting! This man was a very emotionally charged family man, and he completely bonded with me when I told him stories about my kids and family. I make it a point to observe my buyers' gadgets, toys, collections, anything that can give me something to start a discussion about. One of my clients loved Montblanc pens, and I would discuss pens and ink with him before talking shop!

In this age of virtual social media, a great seller doesn't even need to physically meet a prospective client to make a great impression. A few years ago, I vowed to wear all my unique Star Wars T-Shirts every day in an eight-day streak. At the end of the eighth day, I posted my pictures on Facebook. A gentleman called Mandar Natekar observed this and sent me a message on Facebook saying 'You like Star Wars, don't you?' I replied saying, 'Yes!!'. The next day he sent me a full-sized lightsaber of Luke Skywalker as a gift! This was a collector's item, impossible to buy in India. Mandar messaged me saying that he was the head of marketing of an Indian Entertainment TV channel that was broadcasting the Star Wars series and he had received these goodies as gifts from the USA. He wanted me to have the lightsaber because I truly deserved it as a die-hard Star Wars fan. I thanked him and vowed to do anything for him that day onwards! Mandar proved to be the quintessential, killer salesman.

MY LEARNINGS

Selling is a skill acquired by training. It takes oodles of common sense, passion and the love of people and product to make things happen. There are no finite rules of sales. You can invent your own. Awareness above all, is a salesman's best friend.

SPEAKING AND STORY TELLING

From the third grade itself, I was an active public speaker and debater in my school (Campion School at Cooperage in Mumbai). I would participate in all the public speaking competitions possible and would also compete in most inter-school contests. I won top places in these events and that made me rather proud (overconfident) of my skills.

I distinctly remember an inter-school debate competition that I participated in when I was in the ninth grade. The event was in a large auditorium and we were supposed to pick up 'chits' to speak on, just before our turn came. I had never been exposed to this format before and when my turn came to speak, I definitely did not do my best.

Just a few speakers after me, a rather stocky, podgy boy from Cathedral School came on stage. He had an impish smile on his face (which I thought was a bit cocky). But the minute he began to speak, the entire auditorium fell into silence. All of us were awestruck by this super confident boy who was speaking like an authority on a subject that he had been handed just a few seconds ago! He rarely stumbled and went on and on until the bell sounded. Needless to say, this boy won a prize in the competition.

That speaker was Ashwin Sanghi—the famous Indian author well known for many of his books today.

I did not know Ashwin then, but his speech and confidence remained imprinted on my mind forever.

As the years rolled by, I realised that my public speaking and debating skills were extremely helpful in securing speaking opportunities at industry events, conferences and global universities and colleges (including Harvard and Wharton). I discovered that prestigious clients, partners and even investors who were attending those events were intrigued by me and connected with me afterwards. I may not have been able to secure a meeting with them on my own, but because they heard me speaking on stage when they were a part of the audience, they proactively connected with me. That definitely generated lots of new business and lucrative deals. I quickly realised that speaking was a great strategy for being an effective salesman.

All this success also got into my head and I began to believe that I was one of the best presenters around.

A couple of years ago, I hosted my own entrepreneur conference and invited Ashwin Sanghi to speak there. We had got to know each other over the years.

The same Ashwin Sanghi who had floored everyone in the inter school competition thirty years ago, recreated his magic and mesmerised the audience sitting in my entrepreneur conference! Ashwin shared stories, anecdotes, jokes, posed questions, provoked and cajoled us until we were completely smitten by him. I was shocked and awed by the power, aura and impact of his presentation.

Just as Ashwin ended, my daughter sitting next to me, whispered, 'Dad, he killed it. This guy is much better than you.' Never had anyone told me this before!

That moment, I realised how important storytelling was in addition to just speaking and sharing learnings. Ashwin's continued success as a writer and author is an amazing testimony of him being a great salesman and how he is able to communicate, convince, convey and convert his target audience and effectively sell them his tales, and dreams, over and over again.

MY LEARNINGS

A great speaker and storyteller makes a great salesperson. You must practise public speaking. Try and accept as many speaking invitations as you can. If you are are afraid of being on stage, follow my simple trick : When you speak, look directly at the people in the audience, smile at them, engage them, and make them participants in your presentation vs. being silent observers. Do not try to impress or convince them. Just converse with them and tell them stories. As you do this, you will notice how the audience will become your accomplice in your presentation and completely bond with you. You can also look up top presentations made by the global entrepreneurs you idolize and understand their format, style and messaging. You will discover that apart from being masters of their subject, they too are great story tellers—much like Ashwin Sanghi!

LISTENING IS SELLING

One of the greatest lessons I've learned as a salesperson is to be able to listen. People love to talk, and when you give them a patient hearing, they reveal almost everything about themselves, their business, their needs and their challenges. It is very tempting to interrupt them and try and add value to what they are saying, but that's not what they want. They just want someone to listen to them. Also, listening doesn't mean staying mum or losing your tongue; rather it is the ability to speak only when needed or pausing longer than required. Once, in a funding discussion, I was closing out my valuation with a VC when she asked me what number I had in mind. I just kept quiet. The lady also waited for a while. We were playing a 'let's see who speaks first' game. In the end, she spoke up and offered a valuation far richer than I would have proposed! Waiting before speaking paid me rich dividends.

Sales rehearsals

We have all heard of dress rehearsals and the number of times actors need to 'retake' a film shot till they get it right. Many of the millennials I know (including my kids) go to dance and sangeet practices for the wedding ceremonies of their close friends and their family members. The point I'm making is that if so much effort can be expended for a single movie shot or a few minutes of a casual marriage dance performance, why can't we as sellers perfect and rehearse our trade and get our pitch polished to perfection?

In or around the year 2000 when my first startup contests2win.com was growing rapidly in popularity, my PR agency Actimedia headed by Amitabh Saxena and Binita Bodani managed to get me an invite to be a guest in Shekhar Suman's 'Movers and Shakers' show. That programme had achieved near-cult status in India and almost everyone I knew watched it. It was critical for me to make a strong impression on the show personally and for my brand contests2win.com. Many of my potential clients and consumers watched that show. I had to sell myself and come out shining!

As we watched the previous episodes of Movers and Shakers, it was evident that Shekhar Suman liked to get smart with his guests. He would provoke and corner them and always be in command. Amitabh and I discussed his style at length, and we knew that I had to get an edge over Shekhar early on in the show to stay on top, instead of getting squashed by him as it usually happened. I had also to do a great job of selling myself in front of India while keeping Shekhar at bay. One of us came up with the idea of shooting mock video interviews of me getting interviewed. Amitabh acted as Shekhar Suman. As we watched the interview replays, I noticed that my Adam's apple was moving visibly when I got nervous. I was gulping very often. I made a mental note of these so as to correct myself.

A few weeks later, in the show, just after Shekhar Suman introduced me on camera, and began to ask me his typical trick question, I sprung a surprise on him and asked him a Zen riddle. He couldn't answer it and stayed clear of provoking me through the rest of the show. That telecast made me a mini-celebrity and instantly connected Alok Kejriwal and contests2win.com with a large number of consumers and clients. Thanks to that show, people would welcome me when I asked them for meetings and later boast to colleagues saying, 'Hey, you know that guy who recently featured in Movers and Shakers? He came to meet me for business'. An excellent solid sales rehearsal helped me tremendously.

I still remember Sushanto Mitra (my banker whom I mentioned in the chapter 'Knock Knock. Who's there? A VC!') calmly telling me that he was going to make me first pitch my contests2win.com deck to a set of bankers and VCs who were not interested in funding me at all! I was surprised, but Sushanto explained why it was important for me to develop confidence and be prepared for questions that potential financiers could ask. Sushanto was right. The very first genuine pitches I made to investors after my practice rounds were fine-tuned, and they turned out to be good enough to be accepted and funded.

Sometimes, it is also important to 'set the stage' for a perfect sale much like a stage is set in a play to achieve complete audience immersion. If you speak to veteran advertising folks who constantly pitch for new business, they will tell you about the dramatics they plan, curate and execute for a killer client pitch. In my case, Sushanto planned one such coup for me. We were meeting Citibank Private Equity, and it was important for me to impress them. As Sushanto and I discussed the pitch idea, he asked, 'Alok, who are your key mentors and potential board members for contests2win.com? I want them to accompany you to this meeting.' I told him that Cyrus Oshidar of MTV was my creative founder and I was also working with R.Shridhar, the father of direct marketing of India who was with Ogilvy and Mather at that time. Sushanto looked at their profiles and cast the plot. He said, 'Alok, you will be the good Marwari boy with a nice Mont Blanc Ink pen in your formal shirt pocket, complemented with sober dress pants and black shoes. You will give the impression of a solid, serious entrepreneur who is obsessed with driving his business to make money. Cyrus dresses interestingly in real life, so let's invite him wearing a funny T-Shirt and track pants, but tell him to keep his drawstrings hanging out! He will convey the impression of an eccentric, genius, creative Bawa (Parsi). As for Shridhar, let him come in his customary formals with his snow-white beard. Sometime in between the presentation, we will have him stand up and draw all kinds of diagrams and charts on the whiteboard to impress the Citibank team. He will be our Sage of Insights.'

My team and I agreed to follow Sushanto's instructions, and we did exactly as we had planned. It was like 'Alok's 3' going to loot the VC! The Citibank team that met us and heard the pitch was headed by Latika Ahuja, an incredibly sharp and super-intelligent lady. She loved our presentation, ideas and detailed plans to go to market. After discussing my plans at length and grilling me on metrics, Latika did what I had least expected or prepared for. She said, 'Alok, I am fine with the money you are asking for, and the valuation proposed. I am good to go ahead. Shall we shake hands on this deal?' My heart was pounding, and I did not bother to consult with Sushanto. I simply shook her hand.

(I am ashamed to admit here that this was the only deal in my life that I backed out of after shaking hands. After the Citibank meeting, I met ICICI again and was introduced to eVentures. For a variety of good reasons, I closed out my first round of funding with both of them.

I ditched Citibank. I have never gotten over my folly of shaking hands on impulse instead of being patient and waiting before jumping into anything. This deal taught me that.)

MY LEARNINGS

As a salesperson, I have learned to practise, practise, practise till I have become near perfect. When it becomes painful, I think myself as a movie star, getting my 'take' right. If you are starting up, I would advise you to practise your pitch on friends and colleagues and make them object, ask you random silly questions and agitate you. When you go out in the real world to sell, these things are going to happen to you. So practise beforehand.

Finally, remember that when you sell, you not only sell your service or product, but you also sell yourself. Think of the last time you bought something from a dull, snobbish or ill-tempered salesman. Entrepreneurs have to keep selling themselves to VCs, the press, strategic clients, and customers and it's important that they remember the golden mantra: 'Practice makes makes a man perfect.'

BEING INTERESTING

Sometimes, customers just want some good company they can hang out with. I had a client who was the marketing head of a multinational Fortune 500 company based in Delhi. My client loved Mumbai and would travel to the city as often as he could. In the evenings, he had an overwhelming passion for eating at new restaurants. He was neither a drinker nor did he expect to be entertained by me. Despite my best efforts, he always picked up our dinner tab. All he wanted was to spend time with me and talk about tech, ideas, startup life and how I was building my companies. When I brought up the topic of business, he would say, 'Alok, the amount you want me to invest in your website is the advertising budget I spend in a day. Just send me the release order and do an outstanding job with my money. I trust you will not cheat me'.

Once I got talking about western classical music and how I had studied most of the composers and their compositions so deeply that I could recognise almost any classical music playing. I narrated stories about Mozart's childhood to him. My client looked at me and said, 'Alok, this is why I like to meet you. I like your company. You aren't one of those pandering vendors who keep sucking up to me for business. You are a fascinating person, and that's the reason I do business with you.'

Reading voraciously, immersing yourself in passions that interest you outside of work such as sports, art, music, literature can go a long way in building a personality that becomes magnetic and sales friendly. In the early days of contests2win.com, I remember trying to get a bank to sign up as a client. It was challenging because banking was a serious business and the idea of contests and games had limited appeal to the marketing managers in suits and ties making marketing decisions in those banks. I somehow got an appointment with BNP Paribas Bank and met a very nice gentleman called Manoj Namboodiri. He was unsure how we could work together but was decent enough to give me a meeting since I had been harassing him for an appointment. The moment we met, I noticed he was wearing a tie that had Van Gogh's 'Starry Nights' printed on it. I complimented him on his tie and told him how much I admired Van Gogh. Manoj warmed up to me, and over the next few months, we discussed ideas, contesting formats and finally closed on a deal!

MY LEARNINGS

The takeaway is to be original, interesting and genuine. Your demeanour must be everything but that of a seller. That is when you will be able to sell what you want, to whom you want. The more vibrant your personality, the more people will like to meet you, and that will you get more business!

MAXIMISING MEETINGS

When I was in the Class X, I read an article in *Time* magazine that asked Asia's most successful business people to reveal their simple advice for readers to follow. One of the real estate tycoons of Asia's said, 'Keep dealing.'

My interpretation of this was 'Keep selling.' When you make selling your karma, things happen. As a salesperson, you must know everything about the sales funnel. At the top are the clients you meet. As the funnel goes deep, you have strata of clients who are cold, warm, hot, super-hot and converted. Logically, the more extensive the top of the funnel, the more you will sell. This happens when you continuously keep selling.

Another lateral insight I have to share is that when you repeatedly meet customers to sell your offerings, you may chance upon other interesting opportunities to start new business dealings with them.

The period of 2001-2004 was extremely tough for internet companies that had managed to survive the Indian internet bust. Internet penetration was still shallow in India, and convincing clients to create advergames and promotions on websites had become an uphill task. In one such difficult meeting with Jet Airways, their dynamic senior marketing manager Girish Nair told me, 'Alok, you have managed to survive a harsh business environment and convinced so many top clients to do promotions with on your small, yet popular website. The internet itself is such a small-medium in India compared to other media options. Imagine if you could use your skills of creating immersive engagement on the larger platform of Jet Airways! Why don't you become our interactive partner, create exciting promotions for our fliers and start up a new business line for yourself?'

I was charged up, and a few months later, we rolled out an engaging, interactive, monthly promotion that promised high-end prizes to Jet Airways passengers. My team and I were connected to most brand managers in India, and we convinced many top brands to feature themselves on the monthly promotion on board Jet Airways. This product was so successful that it sold for many years without a single break in between. We gave away crores of cars, televisions, holiday trips, mobile phones, Rolex watches and even a Hussain Painting to Jet Fliers as prizes. Of course, we made substantial revenues for ourselves as well. This new interactive format was extended by us to Barista coffee shops in the form of tent cards and with Dominos Pizza Box fliers as well. In the case of Barista and Dominos, the interactive element was responding to the question asked through SMS.

The pattern of reinventing myself and my business kept repeating itself as I continuously kept meeting new clients. While pitching online contests to Ashvini Yardi (now a famous TV show and films producer) who at that time was the creative head of Zee Cafe, I faced a lot of resistance. Ashvini was not convinced that super popular shows like 'Friends' needed promotion! She said, 'Alok, we have more viewers than you. Why should I work with and pay you on top of that?'.

As we brainstormed, I got the opportunity to understand the business of television. While top brands had big budgets to create slick advertising films and buy expensive media on their favourite channels to run their ads, smaller brands with limited budgets just couldn't afford to get on to television. There was an opportunity to garner revenue from niche, local brands that targeted specific consumers such as those who watched American shows like Friends on Zee Cafe. Together, cortests2win.com and Zee Cafe created a brand new format that allowed brands to sponsor prizes for contests on Zee Cafe that got their brand logos on the promotional TV spots! Brands were delighted with this new interactive product that also promised them exposure on television, and many of them signed up with us! Now, contests2win.com was onboard on Jet Airways flights, on tent card in Barista, on Dominos Box fliers and even on television.

MY LEARNINGS

As a seller, I have learned that meeting and engaging large, successful customers on a continuous basis opens up avenues for a lot more business ideas. This does not mean getting distracted from your core value proposition, but if the salesperson is attentive, open-minded and creative, many new ideas can come your way. An advertising Company CEO summarised this very well by telling me, 'Alok, when we sign up clients as their AOR (Agency on Record), we normally don't make a profit on their existing business. However, being the official agency allows us open entry into the client's offices all the time. It is our job as well to land up there every day and keep sniffing for business opportunities we can lay our hands on. Our clients trust us and mandate us to do their extra creative, media and marketing executions instead of constantly hiring and managing smaller agencies. All the extra business put together makes us profitable, per client.' So, if you are starting up, try and spend time amongst large corporations and super-successful startups. You will not only achieve your sales objectives but also get inspired to expand and innovate on your business offerings.

BEING PATIENT

My contests2win.com founding team member Raj Menon (an ace salesman) and I visited the Sony India office (then at Faridabad) to pitch a brand new format of contesting we had conceptualised in collaboration with Jet Airways.

At the Sony office, we met a polite, quiet gentleman called Dinesh Chandra who the marketing manager at that time. After a few pleasantries, I began presenting my pitch which was a short twelve-slide deck. The asking price of the proposal was on slide twelve.

Over the years and after countless sales meetings, Raj and I had trained each other to watch and observe the client as a pitch progressed. We would glance at each other and communicate via subtle gestures and signs.

As I crossed slide nine, I saw Raj reach for his phone. That was a clear signal for me to go slow down. I finished slide ten leisurely. Just as slide eleven came up, I saw Raj's SMS message on my phone. It said 'Do not go to slide twelve. End now.' Just as slide eleven ended, I sat back and thanked Dinesh Chandra for listening. He assumed that the pitch was done.

Just then, Raj pretended to get a phone call, excused himself and stepped out of the room for a minute. Then he came back in, looked at Dinesh Chandra and said, 'Sir, may I borrow Alok for a minute? We have an urgent business matter to discuss'.

Dinesh said 'Sure, no problem. Go ahead.'

The moment we were out, Raj said, 'Alok, Dinesh loves our proposal. I saw his expression. We have asked for Rs 7.5 lakhs on the last slide. He will pay Rs 15 lakhs. Double the price when he asks for the quote'. We came back in and sat down. Dinesh asked me 'So, what does the Jet proposal cost' I confidently said, 'Sir, it costs Rs 15 lakhs'.

Dinesh smiled and said, 'Done. 'Send me the purchase order.'

That was the fastest Rs 15 lakh sale we had ever closed in our lives. Both Raj and I left stunned and ecstatic. When I called Jet Airways and told Girish Nair, our lead at Jet Airways about the sale, he couldn't believe how we had pulled off this sale. Congratulations were exchanged in abundance. In the car, Raj and I smiled at each other and discussed how we had outsmarted Dinesh.

Only a week later did we find out who had outsmarted whom!

It turned out that Dinesh Chandra was launching a brand new range of Sony televisions in India for the first time. A month-long, engaging and interactive contest in Jet Airways that collected an unlimited database of opted-in consumers was the most efficient, targeted marketing Sony India could have ever hoped to execute. Our deliverables were invaluable for Sony India, compared to the measly Rs 15 lakhs we had asked for. Dinesh had outsmarted Alok and Raj, not the other way around.

In retrospect, we think he could have paid multiples of Rs 15 lakh if we had known what he was planning to use the campaign for. But we were impatient and hungry and quick to jump the gun.

MY LEARNINGS

I learned that a great salesperson is never in a hurry and keeps his composure and balance even when things turn out better than expected. A salesperson should deeply understand how his service will benefit his client and price his costs to achieve an equal win for both parties. Thanks to Dinesh Chandra, I realised how silly I was to think that I could outsmart astute professionals who have been in business for years compared to a novice entrepreneur like me who had just started up. Developing a sense of deep respect for your buyers helps in achieving repeated and predictable sales.

Afterword

I was the heir to a large socks manufacturing business that promised me a life of permanent comfort and luxury. Yet, I chose to abandon that business and take the terrifying step of starting afresh, from scratch, by stepping out of my comfort zone. I metaphorically 'stopped wearing my socks'.

Why did I do that?

Because deep inside of me, there was an overwhelming yearning to do something on my own, to chart my own path, and to seek my own fame and fortune.

To do that, I needed to go barefeet first.

Is it easy being an entrepreneur? Of course not! Are people 'born to be entrepreneurs'? I don't believe so. More often than not, people jump on the entrepreneurship wagon impulsively by being overtly influenced by rare success stories they read or because of an acute lack of fulfillment in their jobs and careers. Such entrepreneur stories don't last long. In my opinion, you must find a gigantic problem that is screaming for a solution, it must be a business you thoroughly enjoy and most importantly, begun with a personal commitment of at least ten long years while scaling that venture. Entrepreneurship is not a get-rich-quick card game. That is why I usually advise people to work for a few years, get real life experience and then decide to be your own boss. Having a couple of years' 'survival money' is a great cushion to start with, because entrepreneurship can be a badly paying job, for some years, anyway!

Beyond everything else, you must cultivate the mindset

to be an entrepreneur. All the stories in this book explain some of the pain, agony and mental toughness you need to survive in this marathon called entrepreneurship that has no finish line!

What are the benefits of entrepreneurship? Too many to list down in one place! But let me try anyway. To begin with, it is the path that allows you to pursue your passion and interest and make it a business. It empowers you with the ability to hire people and financially support them and their families. This makes you a direct contributor in building the wealth of the country and to become a key stakeholder in the nation's progress.

Life-changing innovations, and positive disruptions unleashed by entrepreneurs often transform the world and positively help millions of people. Of course, personal wealth and financial strength are important by-products as well.

Does the journey of entrepreneurship ever end? Never! After my first venture, there was was no looking back for me. Post my Mobile2win business exit, I started Games2win and other companies. Entrepreneurs don't retire. They have too much fun doing what they do to give up.

I doubt I will ever wear my socks again!

The question I ask you, dear reader, is: 'When will you stop wearing your socks?'

Acknowledgements

I would like to thank my Mom for always being there for me. My wife, life partner and amazing pillar of support Chhavi for tolerating me all these years and never giving up on me. My school—the Campion School at Colaba and the teachers who taught me, for their amazing guidance in the most formative years of my life.

My school friend Partha Sanyal for inspiring me, Nitin Parkash and his sister Supriya Atal for being one of the earliest believers in contests2win.com.

Jay Zaveri for his amazing support, help and guidance when I was just starting up; my colleague Gaurav Sharma who kept bringing in the sales deals, even in the hardest times; Satish Iyer for being my indispensable CFO, Asha Chaudhry for being my editor for many years; Deeti Dave for her early reading of this book.

My earliest clients including Nanette D'Sa, Ashutosh Tyagi, Nikhil Chand, Shripad Nadkarni, Sargam Bajaj, Sulakshna Pathak, Bhavna Pande, Arun Thadanki, Aparna Chopra, Sandhya Balakrishnan, Yogita Verma, Harshad Jain, Shubhajit Sen, T.Pratap, Shaalu Wadhwa, Neha Lidder, Rajan Patel, Radhika Dhawan, Sanjoy Sen, Sanjay Raina, Manoj Chandra, Unnati Sinha, Ashwin Ramaswamy, Richa Singh, Punyashlok Bhakta, Imraan Surve, Ashwin Deo, Niren Hiro, Ashish Patil, Saurabh Kanwar, Sam Balsara, Miran Shah, Dharmesh Sodah, Shefalii Mahajan Dadabhoy,

Anjali Kapoor for supporting me through my most trying times.

A special thanks to Nilesh Parekh who taught me the fundamentals of accounting and taxation even though I was a clumsy teenager.

My deepest gratitude and thanks to Shri K.V. Kamath and Mrs. Lalitha Gupte who believed in the concept of contests2win.com, trusted me as an entrepreneur and became the first investors in my business.

My utmost gratitude for Sumant Mandal—my investor, guide and lifetime mentor. Thank you for encouraging me to write and allowing me to deeply indulge in my passion.

I am sincerely thankful to my Games2win partners Mahesh Khambadkone and Dinesh Gopalakrishnan who have silently stood by me through the years and tolerated my moods and idiosyncracies.

I am also very grateful to my editor Karthik Venkatesh for his amazing editing, clarity and guidance, without whom this book would not have been possible.